HUNGER ACTION HANDBOOK

Edited by Leslie Withers and Tom Peterson

Seeds Magazine

Chapter 2 is adapted with permission from *Handles for Action*, from the Presbyterian Hunger Program. Chapter 3 is adapted with permission of *Fund Raising Management Magazine*. Chapter 5 is from *Evangelism and the Poor*, ©1986 American Lutheran Church, reprinted with permission of Augsburg Publishing House and ALC Hunger Program. Chapter 12 is adapted with permission of Oxfam America. Chapter 17's section on food is adapted with permission from *Simply Delicious: Quantity Cooking for Churches*, ©1983 by Alternatives. Chapter 24, from *Lives Matter: A Handbook for Christian Organizing*, is used with permission of Sheed & Ward, 115 E. Armour Blvd., Kansas City, MO, phone (800-333-7373).

Single or bulk copies of this book may be ordered from Seeds Magazine, 222 East Lake Dr., Decatur, GA 30030.

1 - 9 copies 7.95 each	*10 - 49 copies 6.75 each*
50 - 99 copies 5.95 each	*100 - 1,000 4.95 each*

Please add 15% to total for shipping and handling. Payment should accompany all orders.

Seeds Magazine
222 East Lake Drive
Decatur, GA 30030

Table of Contents

Acknowledgements

This book represents 10 years of effort as *Seeds* Magazine has shared with its readers practical ways to get involved in the fight against hunger. Besides the co-editors, others from *Seeds'* staff worked on the book: Jan Buckingham—cover design, layout, copy editing and production; Barb Davidson—computer key in; Vic Donham, Evelyn Hodge and Katharine Sederholm—typesetting. Thanks to Gary Gunderson, Seeds' Executive Director, and the other Seeds staff who helped: Susan Caster, Tracy Flynn, Elizabeth Guthrie, Carol Herrick, Sharlene Lee and Shannon Russell.

Seeds as always is grateful to volunteers who proofread and researched chapters: Susan McCarter, Alice Felton, Van Foreman Jr., Rachel Gates, Louise Griffis, Evelyn Hodge, Davis Moore, Bob Nicholson, Nancy-Laurel Pettersen, Theresa Robinson, Patty Woods and Dorothy Young.

A number of other people gave valuable feedback on what should be included. Special thanks go to Colleen Shannon, Presbyterian Hunger Program; George Johnson and Joan Twiton, American Lutheran Church Hunger Program; Myers Park Baptist Church in Charlotte, N.C.; Northminster Baptist Church in Jackson, Miss.; and John A. Conant. Thanks also to Eliza Carney, Eileen Collier, Marty Collier, Vernon Cronmiller, Beth Felner, Andrea Freedman, Wes Hare, Patricia Harrell, Rob Johnson, Ed King, Mel Matteson, Kathryn Palumbo, Jane Remson, Connie Tuttle and Punch Woods.

Introduction

"An ounce of practice is generally worth a ton of theory"
—E.F. Schumacher

This book is for people who want to *do* something, who want to get their hands dirty. It's for those who want to join the tens of thousands of people already on the front line in the battle against poverty and hunger. According to a recent survey, 89 percent of all people living in the United States believe that "wherever people are hungry or poor, we ought to do what we can to help them." The problem is: how? What is the best way to get involved? What can just one person do?.

Many different responses are called for, but no one can do them all. Each of us can decide what we're called to do and do it. *Seeds* magazine isn't offering a blueprint or master plan to end hunger. The chapters in this book are not 24 steps to follow. As long as greed or war exist, food will continue to be another weapon in the scramble for power. While policies of countries, corporations and even churches focus more on short-term gains than long-term needs, poor and needy people will keep falling through the cracks.

But we are not helpless. Over the past 10 years we at *Seeds* magazine have watched, reported and occasionally lent a hand as compassionate women and men have started soup kitchens, shared farming techniques, lobbied Congress, altered lifestyles and taken countless other steps to build a better world. As we share these efforts, we hope that our readers will find something they can do, or ways to improve what they're already doing.

Different types of hunger work do not compete with each other—charity is no more or less important than social change, for instance. Some of us need to be pulling the drowning people from the river while others go upstream and work to prevent people from falling in.

Since hunger is not caused by shortages of food but by people, relationships, especially with poor people, are critical to the effort. Without these relationships, we're in danger of thinking of hungry people as projects. This is not a book of projects. It's about building, nurturing and expanding our caring web of human relationships. People made the problem and people working together can solve it.

The ideas in this handbook have been field-tested by people like you. This handbook describes how to get started as well as to improve an existing program. We hope to answer three comments we frequently hear:

1. Problem? What problem? I don't see any problem!.

Many dedicated people become frustrated when no one seems to care about hunger or wants to do anything about it. As middle-class Americans, we never run into the hungry or homeless people in our favorite shopping mall, nor are we likely to visit the vacant lots, third-world villages or low-income neighborhoods where they live. It's easy to ignore the needs of people we never see. If we want others to feel the problems as urgently as we do, a hunger meal (Chapter 19) or the exercises for knowing the poor (Chapter 5) may be a place to begin. By starting a sister city project (Chapter 11) people in our communities can gain first-hand knowledge of how people live in another country. To involve members of a congregation, the "nine steps" in chapter four or the educational program in chapter 23 may help. For the general public, a good media strategy (Chapter 24) can expand a group's outreach.

2. So many people are hungry! What an overwhelming problem! What can we possibly do?.

More awareness doesn't always bring action. A person can understand that hunger is a daily reality for millions and that the underlying causes of poverty and lack of power are complex and long-lasting and then easily decide that the situation is hopeless and retreat into apathy. Yet each of us can do something. Together we can make a difference!

Working in groups (Chapter 1) can help us overcome feelings of powerlessness, and a community survey (Chapter 6) can help a group find a useful place to begin. For many, raising money to help feed hungry people (Chapters 18 and 22) is an easy and appropriate first step. Some will decide to begin with themselves, volunteering (Chapter 10) or examining the ways we use and share resources (Chapters 15 and 16).

Seeds comes into contact with successful projects week after week. Hundreds of groups across the country have started food pantries, soup kitchens and night shelters (Chapters 7, 8 and 9). Thousands participate in hunger walks (Chapter 21), food drives and community gardens (Chapter 20). As they gain experience and skill, groups become better organized and more efficient. Key areas for many groups are building a financial base (Chapter 3) and nurturing volunteers (Chapter 2). By sharing ideas with each other, we can all learn to do more and do it cheaper and better.

3. The same people keep coming back to us. Their numbers are increasing. They need more than a handout, but our resources are already stretched thin.

While the growing numbers of soup kitchens and other emergency ministries have filled an important need, the volunteers who staff them and the churches, synagogues and other groups that organize and fund them are reaching the limits of what they can do. So we find ourselves turning back to the government, insisting it pick up a fair share of the task. As we work with hungry people, we clearly understand that charity—a helping hand for someone facing crisis—while necessary, is not enough. So, we work for justice, for programs that help people gain skills, resources and power to take care of themselves and their families. That can be changing institutions (Chapter 17) or agencies (Chapter 14) or influencing government policies at the federal level (Chapter 12) or at state and local levels (Chapter 13).

We know we could never cram all that people have learned about how to help hungry people into one book. You'd need a forklift just to carry it around. So we've included information in the appendices to help you find the printed resources, audiovisual aids and organizations that can give you more help.

We will continue to publish ideas for new efforts or new solutions to old problems in *Seeds* magazine. Of course, we want you to subscribe if you haven't already, and we've included a subscription form in the back of the book. We also want you to share the ideas that work for you so we can pass them along to our readers around the country and around the world.

Part One

GET STARTED

The hardest part of practicing is getting the instrument out of the case.

—Jim Smith, Band Director
Spartanburg, S.C. Public Schools

Working to end hunger and learning to play a musical instrument have one thing in common: It's hard to get started. In both cases we need discipline—a deliberate effort to turn old habits and patterns into new ones. Once we're in the habit of seeing the needs of poor and hungry people and responding to those needs, we usually find more and better ways to be helpful. Simply increasing our awareness of the problem can lead to guilt and paralysis. *Acting* on our concern—playing the instrument even though our first attempts are more painful than pleasant—moves us from guilt to responsibility. Habits of active compassion have to be deliberately established.

Musicians set up routine disciplines more easily when others around them are doing the same. Likewise we will be more effective when surrounded with the support and example of others who share our concerns and are acting on them. We don't need to find a hundred committed people before we begin, but we do need a few.

We don't have to be child prodigies to play the piano. Nor do we have to be a saint like Mother Teresa or Dorothy Day to help people. People fighting hunger are just plain folks. Trace the roots of almost any hunger group and you'll find a single, ordinary person with a passionate concern that sparked the compassion of others.

Nor should you wait until you have the perfect plan. All of us see only "through a glass darkly." But each of us can act on the glimmers of light that come to us. If we see and hear poor and hungry people and think and plan with those who share our concern, our vision will be clear and our action effective.

The following chapters give suggestions about how to start and maintain a hunger group. Questions of group dynamics, fundraising, structure and so on are not in themselves a solution to hunger, but effective action seldom happens without paying attention to them. The melody of compassion and the harmony of cooperative action can change the world. But the first step is to take the instrument out of the case.

1

Start A Hunger Group

By Leslie Withers

There are two types of hunger groups: the first exists within a larger organization such as a church, synagogue or school. The second stands alone, perhaps as a non-profit organization.

Both approaches follow the golden rule of hunger work: *Don't do it alone!* Most projects take more than one person, and a group generates more ideas and energy than someone working alone. If a group of people is already doing the work you want to do, don't start something new. Join them!

Take a personal inventory. Ask yourself if you want to serve soup to street people, raise money for wells in an African village, teach people more efficient gardening methods or lobby Congress for programs that help low-income people. Assess your skills and what you'd like to learn.

If no one is already doing what you think is needed in your area, a national organization may be willing to help you get a local project or chapter going. See the appendix for an organization that is already doing that work. If that is a hunger walk, for example, Church World Service/CROP has an organizers' packet, 20 years experience and regional staff to help with local hunger walks. This can save you hours of work and help you avoid preventable mistakes.

We *do* need well-run organizations to help people work together and get the maximum results from their efforts. Brief suggestions for starting a *task group* and an *organization* follow. If you need more help, *Lives Matter* by Kimberly Bobo is an excellent guide to starting and maintaining groups.

Task Group

The simplest organization is one formed for a particular, limited task. It may be as few as three people or as many as are needed to get the job done.

First, find a few other people who share your concern and who want to act on it. Agree on a project and find people who might want to work with you. Limit yourselves to a single project. This may seem frustrating, but remember, no one group can do everything. The clearer the task, the easier it will be to recruit volunteers, raise money and actually accomplish something. A few carefully planned meetings in the beginning can turn a *vast* problem into a manageable project. The four "vast" considerations are:

V for vision. If you don't know where you're headed, how can you work together to get there? Set a goal for yourselves. "Start a soup kitchen in the West End," for instance, is concrete; "Feed street people" is vague. Many groups begin with a brainstorm session then narrow it down to one goal.

A for analysis. Do your homework lest you launch a project that isn't needed or is beyond the group's capabilities. Talk with others who've done similar work. (See chapter 6.) Send for materials and suggestions from a national organization or your denomination's hunger program. (See appendix.) Find out about laws or regulations in your community. Alter your goal, if necessary, based on what you learn.

S for strategy. Plan what is needed to reach your goal and what organizations and people can help you reach it. Determine where the funding will come from. Break the work down into separate pieces that different sub-groups can do.

T for timeline. A step-by-step action plan forces the group to be realistic about its strategy and saves time and energy by putting things in the right order. For each step decide *what* needs to be done, *when* to begin and complete it and, most important, *who* is responsible. The timeline should include meetings to look at what has been accomplished and what remains to be done, so timeline and strategy can be revised as needed.

A Few Hints

Don't worry about numbers! A few dedicated people can accomplish great things with a minimum of organizational hassle. Focus the energy of the people who are there and don't worry about those who didn't show up.

Make sure everyone has something to do. The point of a task force is to do something, not to talk. Encourage everyone to do something that fits or stretches their interests and abilities.

Avoid meeting for the sake of meeting. One person should prepare an agenda that includes reports and decisions to be made. Include an estimated time for each item. Review the agenda at the beginning of the meeting; make needed changes and stick to it.

Keep good, written records. You don't need a full record of every discussion, but everyone does need to know what decisions the group made and who is responsible for implementing them.

Don't let one person dominate the group. Encourage everyone to contribute ideas and be active in the planning as well as in the project. Share the more visible leadership tasks such as chairing meetings or speaking with media.

Nurture one another. People work better together and remain more committed with encouragement and support. The work is important but so are the people doing it. If the group is religious, consider time

11

in your meetings for prayer, Bible study or reflection. A group without a shared religious background may spend a part of each meeting in study and discussion beyond the business of the project. Light refreshments before or after the meeting can provide a setting for informal relationships that are the heart of any well-functioning group.

An Independent Organization

Step one: *Don't do it!—unless you absolutely have to.* The normal American response to a problem is to start an organization to do something about it. Consider the time, resources and hard work it takes to build and maintain the organization. Do you want to spend your limited energy on updating mailing lists, finding a lawyer to deal with incorporation, pricing file cabinets and scrounging typewriters? Or would you rather that energy work directly for hungry people?

Groups that expect to continue for longer than a year or that plan to hire staff or expand beyond the original task should consider a permanent structure. The ideal structure frees the group for the task by establishing routine ways to maintain the organization. To work efficiently over time an organization needs:

A decision-making body. Normally a board of directors takes responsibility for the long-term well-being of an organization and makes important policy decisions. It should represent the people and organizations doing the work. Because the board has financial responsibility for the organization, it also plays an important role in fund raising. (See chapter 3.) At least some board members need to have connections with individuals and organizations that may provide funding. Decide what kinds of representation you need, how members will be chosen, how long they will serve and what their responsibilities will be. One food co-op, for example, expects board members to work three hours a week on co-op business. On the other hand, the board for an annual hunger walk only expects the bishop to involve churches in the walk and to cut the ribbon at the beginning. Each board member should know what to expect when he or she agrees to serve. The board will also need a process for selecting officers and may need standing or temporary subcommittees.

Charter and by-laws. Laws vary from state to state, so consult a lawyer or your state Attorney General's office. Consider both legal requirements and the particular needs of your group.

Tax-exempt status. You need to be incorporated in your state to receive the tax exempt status granted by the IRS. Tax-exempt organizations generally do not pay federal income tax on donations, and supporters may deduct contributions from their taxable income. The question of tax exemption will come up as soon as you begin serious fundraising, so a decision must be made early. Applying for tax-exempt status can be tedious and time-consuming, so unless you plan to raise substantial funds from large donors or foundations you may not want or need to do it. Sometimes a church or another tax-exempt organization can channel designated funds for you instead. Tax laws are in a state of transition and are likely to remain so for several more years, so be sure to seek competent current financial and legal advice.

Staff, office, insurance and other headaches. Think carefully about what is essential to your work. If you can operate just as well out of a shoe box in your basement, don't start a building fund. Keep your goals clearly in mind and tailor the institution to fit them—not the other way around.

2

Nurture Volunteers

By Walter L. Owensby

The only thing harder than getting people involved in hunger work is keeping them involved. Volunteers have a way of wandering away. That's usually not because their hearts have hardened but because they just don't find the work satisfying any more. Here are some reasons why and some solutions.

Burn Out. Most people shy away from organizations that seem poised to eat them alive! Volunteers often leave when they are asked to do too much too soon. To avoid burn-out, we need a series of steps for slowly increasing the responsibilities of new members. Promote them but don't make them chair at their second meeting! Don't ask the same people to work on every task or to work too many hours. Spread the work among existing volunteers or find new ones to lighten the load.

Cool Out. In many groups the number one reason people leave is that they are never asked to do anything at all. "No one asked me to the workshop; no one gave me calls to make; no one seemed to need my help." The solution? Easy! don't be afraid to ask people to help, and don't lose track of people. Touch base with volunteers who missed the last meeting so that doesn't become a reason to miss the next one.

Keep Out. Oldtimers enjoy one another's company and always have business to take care of. That's good, but it too often leaves newcomers sitting alone watching the insiders work. Don't try to legislate against friendship or efficiency. Instead, pair two newcomers in a buddy system and assign an oldtimer to give them basic information. With two buddies to lean on the newcomer won't feel new for long.

Pull Out. When people feel trapped they usually want to get away. Respect the limits people set on their own participation. If they don't like to sell tickets, let them make phone calls. If Wednesday is bowling night, try to find another time when they can help.

Can't Win. Volunteers don't stay if they feel doomed to failure. Communicate the attitude that your goals are worth achieving and that the group can achieve them. Work to set up explicit, short-term objectives and fuss over every success. Don't let people go out on a canvass without a clear standard of how many homes, signatures or dollars constitute

a success, and encourage them to crow about the achievement.
Can't Lose. A sure thing is almost as bad for volunteer staying power
as a lost cause. Fight the anticlimax of success. Connect the victory
in advance to the next steps so that after the celebration volunteers
will have a reason to keep working.

No Growth. Volunteer work should be interesting, offer variety and
give a chance for personal growth. Boring work has to be done in every
organization, but spread it around and include staff. Be sure that those
who want a break from stuffing envelopes have a chance to do some
leadership training or visit your senator.

No Appreciation. Volunteers need to be told often that what they are
doing is important. "Please" and "thank you" are minimums, and ban-
quets are nice. But don't forget to show appreciation by careful attention to details: return phone calls, answer notes, pass along information and schedule meetings volunteers can make.

External Opposition. If family and friends oppose what the volunteer
is doing, odds are you'll eventually lose that person. So make a special
effort to show that the family is "contributing" some of their time with
the volunteer. Find ways and occasions to thank them. Better yet, try
to involve family and friends too. Don't neglect to send the volunteers
home with a steady flow of information showing the usefulness and
importance of the program they are working for. This can help silence
critics.

Internal Conflict. People who share social concerns don't always like
one another. Dealing with conflict depends on the nature of the organization. Some groups mediate the battle; some encourage the bat-
tlers to duke it out; some urge them to make up; and some reorganize
the work so that the combatants won't have to deal with each other
so often.

Policy Disagreements. Sometimes conflict arises over policies rather
than personalities. Volunteers should count in making some decisions,
and time should be allowed for different views to be heard and carefully
considered. The key is to help people feel they have been heard. Most
people can accept losing, but they can't stand being ignored or misunderstood. That's when they quit.

Not Enough Fun. World hunger is serious. But volunteers, and all of
us, need some fun along the way. Don't forget to schedule it in such a way
as to maintain sanity and restore energy. Remember Emma Goldman's
words: "If I can't dance, I don't want to be part of your revolution."

Erratum: In the editing process, the following line was inadvertently
omitted from the first paragraph of chapter 2, Nurturing Volunteers.
It originally appeared in "Handles for Action" and read: "In an
address to a New Jersey nuclear freeze group a couple of years ago,
Peter Bandman noted a dozen reasons why people drop out and suggested
some remedies. Here's a summary of his ideas." Our apologies to both
Peter Bandman and Walter Owensby for this omission. --Editors

3

Build a Financial Base

By Joan Flanagan (adapted)

Popcorn poppers and hot air balloons may run on air but your organization cannot. You will quickly find you need money to sustain your organization. You may also need to raise money for projects to help hungry people. (See chapter 18 for suggestions.) A simple, all-volunteer effort without overhead may have modest financial needs, but serious commitment to long-term work often means setting up an office and hiring staff. That means fundraising.

The first advice for fund raisers, according to grassroots fundraising expert Joan Flanagan, is start today. Don't wait for the "right time." Organizations that are serious and strategic about raising money manage to do it in prosperous times or in hard times, when hunger is highly visible or when it's only on the back pages. If you need money, ask for money. If you want a group to take fund raising seriously, put it first on the agenda of every meeting.

Get the Board of Directors to Raise Money

Ask the board to do more fund raising. If this is a new task for the board, interview each member one at a time. Ask them to tell you about their fund raising for other organizations such as in their churches, clubs, civic organizations, political candidates or labor unions. Ask them to think about where they give their money. At the next meeting ask the board to adapt the ideas they know work to your organization.

The board needs to draw up long-range plans for the next 13 months and then a five-year plan. Long-range plans can help you in the short-term, too. The Everywoman's Resource Center in Topeka, Kansas, projected that its grant money would run out in a year-and-a-half, so they developed a three-part plan to become self-sufficient from membership dues, a special event and a thrift store.

To test the data for the thrift store, the center sold used children's clothing, toys and games in a booth at a weekly flea market. It made a profit, trained volunteers and taught them the resale business. Meanwhile a small business consultant did a study to locate the best site for the store, and a volunteer realtor looked for a store in that area while the center interviewed candidates for the store manager's job. As executive director Cindy Barry says, "The board was committed to the idea of the store so we can make enough money to replace our grants. They get impatient with the planning, but we know it pays off in larger profits in the long run. Since our goal is to replace grant money that runs out, everyone can see how each step fits our timetable."

If the board can't do what needs to be done, start looking for a better board. "Better" means three things: people who are committed to the work of the organization, who give according to their means and who ask for money. To get these people ask for them and keep asking. The president of one board kept asking the same man to join the board for three years. He finally said yes and will be a great addition to the board. To get a better board you may need a better nominating committee. Karl Mathiasen, the dean of Washington, D.C., Non-profit Management Consultants, said, "The most important board committee in any organization is the nominating committee." If you think it is time to improve your board, improve your nominating process. Ask your board to research the organizations they know are flourishing, especially churches and synagogues. Copy the system that produces the best boards.

Remember (and remind the board) that they are legally responsible for the organization's finances, including any debts incurred. The Board (or a subcommittee) should evaluate the fundraising strategy every six months. Calculate the income and expenses for each fundraising activity. Remember all time spent by paid staff is an expense. Then ask a veteran fund raiser to help prepare a written evaluation. Involve as many board members as possible in the evaluation. Remember, the point of the exercise is to find ways to make your fund raising better: more dependable income, more volunteers, more fun. The question to ask is: "How can we make more money in less time next year?"

The Board can also involve more people. This is always the right answer to your evaluation question. If you want more money from dues, double your membership committee, or triple it. If you want more money and much more fun from your special event, double the committee and cut the time in half. It will be easy to get volunteers next year.

Never give up. Last year the *New Yorker* profiled Knud Jenson, founder and director of the Louisiana Museum in Denmark. At one point Jenson remarked with a sigh, "Sometimes it takes herculean strength to maintain the optimism of my board." I'm sure we've all felt that way! It may seem easier to do the work yourself than instill courage and confidence in the board that will make them succeed.

Go Back to the Same People Again

Keep systematic records of individuals and organizations that have supported you in the past. This is your funding base—those you count on to sustain the organization. Computers can make this a practical task and maybe a competent volunteer can help set up a system.

Ask donors regularly for more. The best people to ask for money are people who have already given you money. They have invested in your work, so ask them again and again. Churches get the lion's share of the philanthropic dollars in the United States (46.3 percent in 1981) because they ask for money 52 times a year. If they can ask 52 times, you can ask two, three or four times or more.

Consider a pledge system for your most faithful givers. It will conserve valuable staff time and resources and provide a regular, monthly source of funds. In the fall ask everyone who has given a substantial sum or has given more than once to consider a monthly pledge for the coming calendar year. Send each person who agrees a year's supply of return envelopes and a post card reminder once a quarter. You may wish to call people who are more than a month behind. Ask if they need to change their pledge. Next fall ask all pledgers to renew their pledge for a higher amount, and ask new large donors to consider pledging.

Your clients can help with fund raising. They are getting the benefits of your work, so who is more qualified to explain how wonderful you are? In 1982 the CHART job training agency in Minneapolis launched its first phon-a-thon. It was modeled after the typical college campaign where students call alumni, but in CHART's case the agency's current clients volunteered to call its 1,800 most recent alumni. In three nights they raised $3,500.

Marion Etzwiler, executive director of CHART said, "We learned a lot, and our people loved doing it. We got some excellent free advice to improve our programs and plenty of compliments on our work. Many women gave money in warm response to the call. One woman sent $100 with a note saying, 'When I went through CHART, you gave me a scholarship. Now I want to help another woman go through.' Another woman's note said, 'Here's $2, all I can give. I wish it was more.'"

The best lesson they learned was to start farther back on their alumnae list. Women who had graduated in the last year gave the least because their lives were still in transition, and they had just paid a fee to CHART. Fortunately, the women who had been out for more than a year were making money and eager to give when asked by a current client.

Churches and synagogues can be sustaining supporters also. Rather than asking a congregation to take up a special offering, ask them to write your group into the annual budget. Once they agree, a short, simple request each year will remind them that you still count on their support. If you draw volunteers from the congregation, have a board member from the congregation or provide them with programs or educational resources during the year, they will be even more likely to respond favorably. Before making your first request to a congregation, find out what their budget process and deadlines are. Also find out whether committees, such as the Social Concerns Committee, have their own budgets to support outside causes. Keep careful records, and the following years' requests can become routine.

Don't Give It Away

Ask people to pay a fee for your services. For example, CHART offers services in job information, personal growth and career planning. Most similar organizations offer that information free, but in 1982 CHART raised $192,000 in fees, 43 percent of its budget.

Make a sliding scale for fees. You have to be realistic in your fund raising. Some people are not working or did not get a raise last year. Let them have a bargain. On the other hand, not everyone is poor. For example, St. Luke's Episcopal Church runs a counseling service in Atlanta. Their fee is based on the person's annual income, so they get from $1 to $70 per hour. Although most people report an annual income of $5,000 to $20,000, they have helped people with incomes of $200,000 and more. A sliding scale gives you a fair way to charge everyone who can help.

Try to make every activity a moneymaker. If your paid staff now does public speaking free, ask for an honorarium. Even better, create a "Speakers Bureau" run by volunteers and change a money drain into a money maker. Re-examine everything you give away now: publications, services, training, advocacy. Ask "How can this make money?" Put a price on all of them. You will quickly get a free, accurate evaluation of which are good enough to pay for and which are not. Discontinue the junk, and market the best work.

Keep Costs Down

Be serious about cutting costs. Involve all the staff in thinking of ways to save. At one agency a businessman called to offer two free typewriters. The switchboard operator said they didn't need them but recommended another non-profit that did. Unfortunately the organization did need them desperately, but she didn't know it because the boss thought telling the staff the true financial picture would weaken morale. (Another way of saying, "They will think I don't know what I'm doing.") Honesty is always the best policy inside your agency. Give weekly reports in tight periods and make everyone part of the cost-cutting team. Lavish praise on anyone who finds a way to save money.

Cooperate with similar groups. Look for ways to share equipment, office or meeting spaces and paid staff. Most of all, cooperate in your fund raising efforts. You will all make more money. In Tucson, Arizona, the Food Bank and the Hunger Action Center jointly sponsor a hunger walk each year. Because they provide very different services (wholesale food and education about hunger) and have different constituencies, the combined walk attracts more people and raises more money than either could alone.

Diversify Your Sources of Money

Plan to bring in the majority of your budget from grassroots money:

19

dues, pledges, corporate gifts, major donations, special events and dependable year-round moneymakers such as bingo or door-to-door canvassing. Then add money from sources you cannot control such as foundations, the government and the United Way.

Diversify your income from every special event. (See chapter 18.) Sell T-shirts at the Hunger Walk. Invite people to pledge at the benefit concert. Promote your calendars and note cards the next time you bring in a speaker from out of town. Sell advertising space in the program for the banquet.

In-kind contributions can stretch your budget enormously. The key is to know exactly what you want. Ask for it and you'll get it. Vinita Ricks, a volunteer for Family Rescue, a battered women's shelter on Chicago's South Side, went to the neighborhood Sears store and got a free kitchen. Volunteers went to Sears first and researched their appliances. Then Vinita was able to ask for each one by size and model number. They got a 23 cubic foot freezer, a 19 cubic foot refrigerator for upstairs, a 13 cubic foot refrigerator for downstairs and a stove. As Gay Northrup, director of Family Rescue, says, "The only thing we didn't get exactly like we wanted was the stove because we didn't have the model number."

Ask a church or synagogue to donate office space. Go to local labor unions with requests for donated, skilled labor: electricians, truck drivers, plumbers. Use your newsletter to let supporters know you need another typewriter or file cabinet. Be sure to list in-kind contributions as well as cash donations in your financial statements, so other potential donors will have an accurate picture of the group's financial support.

Ask foundations for more than charity. Rob Collier, program officer of the Charles Stewart Mott Foundation, has counseled fund raisers, "Foundations can make your life easier. Ask them for technical assistance to help with retrenchment or suggestions for collaboration with other groups. Most of all, foundations can help you clarify your planning." Since they know hundreds of organizations, ask them for advice and for introductions that will help you make more money. The Peace Development Fund, for instance, holds regular workshops in fundraising and organizing as well as giving grants.

Meet Real Needs

Sophie Ann Aoki, political and training director of Citizens Campaigns, Inc., supervises the operation of its professional door-to-door fund raising canvasses. In 1982 their 15 canvassing offices made $2.7 million. Ms. Aoki says, "There is a serious need for action on problems people are facing. If a canvass relates to organizations that work on problems people care about, the canvass is successful." People will always give money to a representative of an organization that gets results on the issues they care about. In fact, this may be America's oldest form of fund raising. Historian Barbara Mayer Wertheimer recounts that while George Washington's soldiers were starving and dressed in rags in 1782, "Women went door-to-door collecting supplies, money, medication, food and pewter to melt for bullets. They accepted any contribution that could be put to use."

Finally, have the courage of your convictions. Ask for large amounts. Believe in your organization, your leadership, your purpose and yourself. And do it now. As Will Rogers said, "Even if you're on the right track, you'll get run over if you just sit there."

4

Involve Your Congregation: 9 Steps

By Leslie Withers

1. Study the Bible.

Active congregational study, prayer and worship related to the real world are the foundation of a faithful response to hunger. Encourage members to examine the scriptures. Develop a one-year plan that involves every age group in exploring how the Bible and other teachings of our faith relate to problems of hunger and their solution. (See chapter 23 on how to educate your congregation.)

2. Find out what your denomination or religious group is doing.

Almost all have channels for hunger response as well as materials for hunger education. Don't duplicate what already exists. See the Appendix for denominational hunger programs.

3. Enlist disciples.

Identify members of the congregation who are ready to respond with faith and enthusiasm to the challenge of hunger. Avoid thinking only of people who worked on social concerns last year. Perhaps they will be part of the core group, but limiting your group is harmful to them and to the congregation. (See chapter 1 for suggestions on starting a task group.) Anyone is capable of responding in faith and is a potential member of the task force. According to a recent survey most volunteers began when someone they knew asked them to help. Be bold and believe the good news: God calls each of us to the exciting work of building a better, more just world.

4. Study your own community.

Discover what hunger problems exist in your area and what local groups and churches are doing. Send small groups to listen to people who hurt, who struggle, who silently suffer from poverty. Study how your congregation can add its energy to work already being done or begin needed work no one else is doing. (See chapter 6 for more hints on community surveys.)

5. Develop a plan.

The core group's job is to plan goals and strategies for the congregation. Name one person as the hunger contact person and coordinator in your parish. Develop a plan for the first year and an outline for the next three years. Study the hunger material from your denomination but work ecumenically if possible. Include in your plan Bible study, education on root causes, fund raising, involvement with the poor and advocacy efforts with suggestions for each age group.

6. Encourage regular giving.

People give generously if they have current information and are asked specifically. Sharing financial resources is often the first response to hunger. Place hunger envelopes in pew racks and have monthly ones put in your box of pledge envelopes if appropriate. Support your denomination's hunger appeals as well as hunger walks and other ecumenical fund raising activities. Some will respond to the challenge to give one percent of their income to the poor and hungry.

7. Use your citizenship.

Our votes and our voices count in our democracy. To advocate public policy that helps the poor and hungry is part of our witness as people of faith. Encourage members to stay informed and to write elected officials about hunger issues. Letter writing is something every age group can do. (See chapters 12 and 13 for more suggestions on advocacy with federal or state and local elected officials.)

8. Examine your lifestyle.

Good stewardship of your personal and group resources is a positive response to hunger. People look for ways to break free from the captivity of materialism, greed and wasteful living. Offer alternative ways to celebrate, shop, transport, entertain and cook. Don't forget your congregation's corporate stewardship, including use of the building, food served, etc. (See chapters 15 and 17 for suggestions.)

9. Don't forget to celebrate.

To remain hopeful and positive while hunger persists, celebrate the presence of God. The renewal that comes through regular worship and group celebration keeps the vision alive and builds community. Learn to celebrate the gift of food. Use drama, music, clowning, dance and puppets. Share success stories that keep hope and courage alive.

Part Two

Meet Your Neighbors

To us, what matters is an individual. To get to love the person, we must come in close contact with him. We ourselves feel that what we are doing is just a drop in the ocean. But if that drop was not in the ocean, I think the ocean will be less because of that missing drop.

—Mother Teresa

Every major world religion has a golden rule about loving others as you love yourself. Most hunger workers would say they're motivated by love, compassion or concern. Yet abstractly loving someone we don't know usually doesn't last long or result in much.

Stepping into the lives of the people we want to help can be frightening, depressing or even dangerous. To be honest, some people who wander into a soup kitchen are not easy to love. A night spent in a shelter with homeless people or in the bamboo shack of a poor peasant family can put us out of kilter with a society that wants to keep the poor out of sight and out of mind. But when we meet the poor, we begin to understand that—if only given the chance—most people will solve their own problems. What we gain from those we would help is equal to, if not greater than, anything we can give them. Myths about each other are dispelled and barriers begin to come down.

True help is based on relationship. Through *Seeds* magazine we meet people who have done some pretty amazing things: the farmer who returns from a short voluntary mission to India to become a powerful catalyst for change in his community; the church secretary who starts a soup kitchen with $10; the preacher who is distressed to find his South Georgia neighbors living in shacks and begins a small project that eventually builds thousands of homes around the world. Each of them was able to help because they knew and understood the people they were helping. In building those relationships they also grew themselves. People working in a soup kitchen or volunteering overseas find strength and satisfaction that armchair experts never experience.

5

Get to Know the Poor

By George Johnson

Before we can respond to the needs of poor and hungry people with compassion and integrity, we need to know them as people. Avoiding poor people is easy in our culture, but even people who want to reach out may find themselves blocked by fear or lack of information. One way for a group to overcome these obstacles is to ask each member to commit themselves to one of the following actions. When the group shares their experiences and what they learned, they will be better able to decide on long-term work they wish to do. Here are some suggestions for meeting poor people and learning about their needs.

Volunteer to help at a food pantry or soup kitchen two times during the next four weeks. Enter conversations with the recipients.

Volunteer with others to weatherize the home of a poor family or elderly person and get to know the residents.

Volunteer to serve and/or observe at an emergency center for the poor. Examples might include the emergency waiting room at your county hospital, the courthouse where hearings and trials take place, the food stamp center or the legal aid office.

Visit the unemployment office on two different occasions and talk with applicants.

Volunteer twice to accompany a social worker or police officer on visits to the poor in order to better your understanding of their struggles.

Spend one night from 10:00 p.m. until 5:00 a.m. on the streets of an inner city to listen, touch, taste, smell and feel how some people of our society live. (This should be done in pairs or as a group.)

Go on a short trip to a third world situation where face-to-face encounter with the poor is made possible.

Arrange for two visits with a refugee or displaced family, one in your home, one in their home, to discuss their struggles, culture, values and signs of hope.

Volunteer to spend a night at an emergency shelter or halfway house and listen to the stories of those who need this service.

Visit an Indian reservation and arrange for in-depth conversations with Native Americans and those who work with them.

Visit a prison on two different occasions and enter into dialogue with inmates with a special focus on poverty, racism and societal prejudice.

Visit with two farm families who have faced foreclosure. Seek understanding and give support.

These suggestions are from the study guide *Evangelism and the Poor: a Biblical Challenge for the Church.* (See appendix.) Going through the five study sessions can help a group use the above experiences to deepen their understanding, commitment and ability to respond to the poor.

Survey Your Community

By Leslie Withers

When considering new hunger work in your community, your group can gain valuable information and insights with a simple survey. Some groups use rigorous studies with statistically valid methods to convince government officials that new public programs are needed. Such a survey, though valuable, requires technical expertise and is beyond the scope of this book. You can get more information about this kind of survey, usually called a "needs assessment," from FRAC at the address in the appendix. Or contact Laurie True with the Northern California Hunger Action Coalition: 1900 K Street, Suite 200, Sacramento, CA 95814. Tel. (916)446-7904. They've helped several California groups do needs assessments that are beginning to have a substantial impact on state and local legislation there.

A simpler survey done by lay people with a minimum of training can direct your local group toward needed projects. Its purpose is to gain an informal understanding of hunger and nutrition problems in your community and what is already being done. You will also establish relationships with local service agencies and organizations and determine whether a new project is needed or whether your group should volunteer to support an existing program.

Preparation

First decide whether the scope of the survey will be limited to food-related needs and services or include broader issues of poverty such as housing and health care. Define the boundaries of your community. Find the programs and organizations that provide services in your target area with address, phone number, office hours and a contact person for each. Check the telephone book, your local library or a guide to services provided by the United Way or another helping agency in your community for these programs:

1. The *Special Supplemental Food for Women, Infants and Children (WIC)* program provides high protein food to pregnant women, new mothers and young children who cannot afford an adequate diet. This program is administered through your state Health Department.

2. The *Food Stamp Program* is administered on the state level through the Department of Human Resources or Social Services. Each county usually has at least one certification office.

3. *Elderly Nutrition Programs* provide hot meals at designated places or for delivery to home-bound senior citizens. These programs are administered through the state office for the aging or department of senior citizens.

4. *School Lunch and Breakfast Programs* are administered through the State Department of Education. Inquire through your local school board or school administration office.

5. The *U.S. Department of Agriculture's Food and Nutrition Service* regional offices may provide food for children in organized childcare programs, advice for low-income families on preparing low-cost, nutritious food or other food-related assistance.

7. If your community has a *Food Bank,* most groups that run soup kitchens or other feeding programs will be registered with it, and it can tell you the ones that serve people in your area. To find the Food Bank nearest you contact Second Harvest at the address in the appendix.

8. Check with the Salvation Army, church or social service groups with soup kitchens and food pantries as well as hunger coalitions or interfaith food task groups.

To look at other poverty-related problems check the Employment Security Division. It provides counseling, job services and training for unemployed people. Look for public health clinics, migrant farm worker services, legal aid offices, veterans organizations and public housing tenant organizations.

After gathering this background information set a date to complete the survey. To calculate the time needed consider the number of surveyors and the number of organizations to be visited. Assign two-member teams to visit one or more agencies. You may need to recruit additional volunteers: retired people, students on vacation or others who can get to weekday appointments. If possible, pair new recruits with someone familiar with the group's plans and needs. Instruct each team on how to introduce themselves and conduct the interview. Make sure they know what questions to ask, how to take notes carefully and how to make a written report.

Conducting the Interview

Each team first sets up its assigned appointments. Allow 30 minutes for an interview and enough travel time to arrive promptly. Introduce yourselves, explain why the survey is being conducted and listen attentively. Take careful notes and write down key statements word by word. Express your appreciation at the end of the interview. Important questions include:

- What does your program do?

- Who is it designed to help?
- How do people learn of the program?
- How many are currently being helped? What percentage of eligible people receive services?
- Why are others not participating?
- Do you know of people who are hungry?
- Do you know how many in our area suffer because of hunger and poor nutrition? Is the problem getting worse or better?
- What would happen if this program did not exist?
- How could our group help meet the needs you see as most critical?
- Do you have other comments or suggestions concerning poverty and hunger in our area?

Followup

Each survey team should send a thank-you note and, if possible, a written copy of the survey results to each person visited.

Meet to share and evaluate the results of the interviews and make plans based on what has been learned. If your staff or volunteers have time, compile all the group reports into one written summary and distribute it ahead of the meeting. When you get together, follow these steps:

- Ask people to share the most important one or two things they learned. Note major points on newsprint or chalkboard.
- Summarize key information about each agency on newsprint or chalkboard: Where services are available, for whom they are available and additional help needed.
- Look for major gaps in meeting community needs.
- Discuss what you learned about the effect of reduction and expansion of government programs on community services. How are church-related and private programs affected?
- Ask whether surveyors got a sense of what it would actually be like to seek aid and how they felt about it.
- How could existing programs be improved?
- List possible group projects based on what you've learned.

The group's first reaction may be overwhelming frustration and discouragement at the discovery of so many urgent needs. It's a normal, healthy reaction. The needs are usually beyond the ability of any single organization or individual, but you don't have to remain paralyzed. The point of the survey is to find an area where needs are not being met where your group can help. You may need more than one meeting but try to list possible projects in the first meeting after the survey. That gives people an opportunity to think about the list before deciding on a single project. Don't try to do everything, but look for one specific task that motivates your group and will be of real use to poor and hungry people in your community.

7

Start a Food Pantry

By Gail Olsen

Food pantries can be a good place to begin direct service to the poor for those who have never been exposed to poverty. Volunteers may only donate cans of food now and then, or they may give valuable time to the pantry.

Sometimes a single congregation or civic group will start a pantry, but often several work on it together. Thus, the first step is to create a task force with representatives from the groups that will operate the pantry. (See chapter 1 for hints on starting hunger groups.)

The task force should first examine the community's needs. (See chapter 6 for suggestions on doing a survey.) Before starting a food pantry find out if an existing one already meets those needs. If so, can you simply work with that organization? A survey will also introduce you to helpful social service agencies that can provide guidelines for policy and help train volunteers. Agencies often employ public relations people to assist organizations like yours. Respect their expertise, and they will respect your commitment.

Ask representatives from agencies like Aid to Families with Dependent Children (AFDC), Red Cross Information and Referral Service, United Way and the Salvation Army to meet with your task force. If they are busy, meet them in their office. Tell them clearly that you don't want a speech but specific information to use in planning a food pantry. People who run food pantries similar to the one you are planning can be especially helpful.

The task force needs to make important policy decisions about who to help and the extent of the help offered. Some basic ones are:

Screening Applicants. Remember that the reason for all this work is to deliver food to those who need it. So try to avoid unnecessary hassles for applicants while protecting the system from gross abuse. Many people, however, are concerned with those who make the rounds of churches searching for handouts. Though their number is small they can sour people against helping all the rest. If this is a concern in your community, you may want a screening system. If possible, have one or two people deal with all applicants for consistency and fairness.

Some food pantries ask referral services like the Red Cross or the food stamp agency to screen for them. Provide them with a copy of your policy, and they will send only those who meet your eligibility requirements. Make up referral slips, and instruct volunteers staffing the pantry to accept only people who have a slip signed by an authorized agency representative. A simple slip might look like this:

Date _____

This is to introduce _____

In need of _____ days of food

for _____ adults and _____ children.

Is baby food needed? _____ Special diet needs? _____

Authorized signature _____

I have received the above food

Client _____

On the other hand, a referral system may cut you off from the needy. The point of the pantry is to help people, not to see how little food can be given.

Limits. Decide how long you will feed one family. If you plan to supply food until they receive emergency food stamps, allow for holidays and weekends. Take the time to understand the other aid systems your pantry is supplementing so that you can be truly useful. Decide the number of visits any one person can make to your pantry. Many pantries limit clients to one three-day supply of food per month.

Type of Food. The kinds of food to be given will determine the equipment you need. (For example, fresh foods require refrigeration.) Home-canned items may not be properly prepared, so only accept commercially canned goods. Check with the health department to see if they allow repackaging items like pinto beans and rice. Most items cannot be repackaged, and boxed items should be unopened. Think about what you would want. Non-food items such as shampoo, detergent or disposable diapers are useful since they cannot be bought with food stamps.

From Shelves to Hands. If clients pick up food at the pantry itself, you will need to maintain regular, publicized hours. Volunteers should be assigned specific hours to keep the pantry open, or participating groups can take turns providing staff on regular days. If you deliver food, you will need a telephone contact system with a number that can be widely published. The contact could be someone who is usually home, perhaps a shut-in. Or "call forwarding" could direct calls to the appropriate phone. After taking the request the contact person calls a volunteer who delivers the food from the pantry. The delivery person needs to know how to help the families in ways that protect their dignity.

Who is Responsible? Plan now for the continued operation of the food pantry. If it is not a program of a single organization, consider setting up a board of directors. Will your task force become such a board? How will new members be selected? Schedule regular meetings and keep records of decisions.

Design a plan of operation complete with mechanisms for change. For example, will change come by consensus or by vote? Before final adoption, ask for input from ministers, social workers and volunteers from other pantries to help clarify areas misunderstood or overlooked. Involve religious and community leaders. It helps ensure their support when you ask for contributions.

Legalize your good intentions.

Check the legal requirements that apply to your food pantry. A lawyer may volunteer advice and time. Different rules apply to nonprofit voluntary organizations than businesses, and every community has different laws. Contact the department of health for a license and the regulations on dispensing food. Your local foodbank probably has standards for groups that receive food from them. Seek good advice on setting up your checkbook so all donations can be recorded and documented.

Select a name for the pantry.

Words like "food" and "kitchen" give a positive image, while "hunger" denotes need. If the pantry is an all-Presbyterian or all-Catholic effort, you might put that in the name. Be creative but not weird—you will live with the name a long time.

The Food

The simplest supply of nourishing food is a pantry stocked with canned and prepackaged dry foods that still includes choices. Stock food that your clients will find both healthy and attractive.

Find out if there is a food bank nearby. Second Harvest, listed in the Appendix, can tell you about the bank nearest you. Food banks make good salvaged food available to non-profit groups.

Seek local advice on what specific items are best to stock. Food pantries in Knoxville, Tenn., give a three-day supply of food recommended by a nutritionist, an agricultural extension agent and a food pantry director. Substitutions are based on availability and cost. Lists describe the amounts needed according to family size. For a family of four, their three-day food box looks like this:

dry orange drink mix 8.8 oz.
dry milk, 5 qts.
cream of wheat, 14 oz.
tomato soup (2 cans), 10 oz.
chicken noodle soup (2 cans), 10 oz.
vegetable soup (2 cans), 10 oz.
peanut butter, 18 oz.

cut green beans (2 cans), 16 oz.
pork and beans (2 cans), 16 oz.
mixed greens, 15 oz.
spaghetti with meat sauce (2 cans), 16 oz.
applesauce (3 cans), 16 oz.
fruit cocktail, 16 oz.
peaches, 16 oz.

saltines, 1 lb.	corn bread mix, 8 oz.
macaroni dinner, 7 oz.	tuna, 12 oz.

Keep all food on shelves off the floor and protected from vermin and moisture. A small 7 x 9 foot room with shelves on the walls should be adequate. Keep it simple and logical. If you can repackage them, dry beans can be stored in large seamless plastic cans (new garbage cans are ideal). Boxes can be stored in plastic bags or the refrigerator. .

Getting Donations.

You will need donations of money, food, time and specific items such as shelving, refrigerators and a sign. Tell churches and civic clubs your specific needs. Many people will help if you tell them what you need. Don't ask for "volunteers," ask for "two people to help put up shelves at 10 o'clock Saturday morning."

If you ask for food, be specific. For instance, ask for commercially canned corn, peas, peaches and one-pound bags of flour. Otherwise you will get perishable items and 100 pound sacks of flour, artichoke hearts, gefelte fish, bubble gum and home-canned rutabagas. Encourage people to donate money because cash used to buy food from wholesalers or the food bank goes farther than if the donor buys food at retail prices. (See chapter 20 on collecting food.)

Plan a "grand opening" and publicize the date. Use the announcement to remind congregations and organizations of your financial needs. The need to stock the shelves before opening gives your appeal urgency.

Training.

Volunteers will need training in several areas. They should be able to help with meal planning and know the right amount of food for various-sized families. The number and age of children is an important consideration. Different menus are required for families with and without cooking facilities or refrigerators. Tastes vary among ethnic groups. Ask a nutritionist to prepare a number of sample menus that can be adjusted to fit the situation. Volunteers who deal directly with people coming for food should develop skills and sensitivity to clients' needs as well as the ability to refuse unreasonable requests or requests outside the pantry's guidelines. Finally, training should also familiarize staff with the other agencies and systems your clients will be dealing with such as the food stamp program and AFDC.

Looking Down the Road.

Once the food pantry is operating efficiently, continuing publicity builds interest and stimulates a regular flow of canned goods and money. Monthly reports to supporting groups will personalize your service. Don't simply give raw numbers—40 families, with an average of 2.3 children. Relate a short story: "Father lost his job due to layoffs and needed food while awaiting food stamps for his wife and four children. The kids were ages 11, 9, 6, and 2." While the names of the indigent families must remain anonymous, the names of volunteers should be published. Get quotes from them about what helping others has meant to them. Take every opportunity to thank volunteers and supporting organizations, and keep referral agencies aware of your progress. They will appreciate your professionalism and be a source of valuable advice.

Successful operation of a food pantry can become a stepping-stone for further involvement. As stories of individual hardship and problems surface, assistance may be broadened to include help completing food stamp applications or referral to social service agencies such as Legal Aid or family counseling. Your volunteer pool may include people with expertise in nutrition, law or budgeting, for instance, who will share their knowledge with those in need. Let the obvious need for food be a prod to awareness of other human needs.

8

Start a Soup Kitchen

By Susan McCarter

Soup kitchens used to be associated with the Great Depression or the Salvation Army's work on Skid Row. Today soup kitchens provide refuge and a hot meal for tens of thousands of the "new poor," the working poor, the unemployed and the unemployable. For those who serve, soup kitchens provide an opportunity to exercise compassion and to learn from and about poor people.

Many churches, synagogues and other organizations, particularly in urban areas, provide daily hot meals—the only meal each day for some. No two programs are the same. Needs are different and so are neighborhoods. Methods of getting food, funds and volunteers vary and so do menus and serving times. Some soup kitchens pay their staff while others are all volunteer.

Before deciding to start a soup kitchen, assess the need in the immediate neighborhood. People unable to buy food rarely have cars or bus fare so the kitchen must be within walking distance of the people it will serve. Another problem, particularly in smaller towns, is potential guests' fear that friends and neighbors will see them waiting in the soup line. "Gentrified" neighborhoods pose a special problem: Poor people may gather there, but businesses or residents want them to move on.

Before starting a kitchen find out if another soup kitchen is nearby. If so, visit it, volunteer and ask questions. Make sure the need is greater than their capacity. Then look at your kitchen and dining area. How well equipped is the kitchen? Are there large pots for soup, freezer space for large quantities, plenty of trays and pitchers?

You don't need thousands of dollars to start a soup kitchen. St. Luke's Community Soup Kitchen in Atlanta began when a volunteer receptionist at St. Luke's Episcopal Church confided to her prayer group that she could no longer afford to work there one day a week because after she had given out all 10 meal tickets provided by the church, she spent everything in her purse to help the hungry who came to the door. Another member of the group exclaimed, "I can feed 50 people with what the church spends for meal tickets."

And so it began. Each night she made a pot of soup at home, and others made peanut butter sandwiches for Atlanta's "street people." Today, ten years later, between 700 and 900 people are fed daily. The menu consists of soup, two sandwiches, coffee and dessert. St. Luke's is a "faith operation" that uses what is donated and buys only what is needed to round out the meal.

Not all soup kitchens are in churches, but for those that are, the support of the congregation is critical. Church leaders can teach and preach the scriptural basis for feeding the hungry and encourage members to support this ministry with their time, prayers, money and food donations. Staff can help strengthen weary volunteers, train those who have never before been exposed to this level of poverty and provide occasionally needed discipline to keep an unruly guest in line. Your pastor's enthusiasm will help establish the necessary base of congregational support. Some church members will feel threatened by soup kitchen guests, and pastoral support can keep the soup kitchen from becoming a source of strife and dissension in the church. If the soup kitchen is not the project of a church, be sure you have backing from an organization such as a civic club or school, from a coalition of groups or from an independently created organization. Long-term commitment is critical, or the kitchen is unlikely to outlast the first flush of enthusiasm.

The Leadership Team (Working Group)

The group can be informally organized in the beginning. Areas of responsibility could be filled by one person, but some will eventually require subcommittees.

Meal Planner/Cook: Plans menus and, if not actually cooking, provides recipes and menus for the cook. Most soup kitchens plan around donations and buy only what they must to round out the meal.

Treasurer: Responsible for money donations, ordering and paying for food and supplies and maintaining an inventory. May form a "scavenging committee" to locate sources of money or food.

Secretary: Keeps minutes of all meetings, writes appeal letters and thank you letters to donors.

Publicity Chair: Sends information regularly to newspapers, county or city government agencies, churches and other organizations that aid the poor.

Volunteer Coordinator: Recruits and trains volunteers. Appoints, supervises and coordinates "day captain" for each day the kitchen is open. The day captain coordinates the volunteers, assigns tasks and works closely with the cook so the system operates smoothly.

Overall Director: Responsible for coordination and supervision of the cook, the volunteer coordinator and the day captains. Whether the director is a paid staff person or a volunteer, one person should be clearly in charge.

Planning Ahead

Once the working group is established and functioning as a team, the next step is planning and policy-making. Essential decisions include:

Type of Menu and Service. Some soup kitchens serve hot casseroles prepared in volunteers' homes. Others serve only soup and sandwiches. Some prepare casseroles on the premises the day before and cook them early the next morning. A consistent type of menu simplifies meal planning, food buying and the use of volunteers.

Some groups take bag lunches to places like city parks where homeless people gather. Some feed as many people as possible in shifts at tables in a church basement. Still others use no lines, but serve guests at cloth covered tables with flowers.

Screening/Eligibility. Will you serve everyone who comes in or screen for need and/or eligibility? A soup kitchen without screening is more efficient. Feeding an occasional freeloader is a small price to pay for a generous, welcoming atmosphere that eases the pain of being dependent on others.

Quantities. Consider setting limits on how much food to serve until experience shows how much is available. However, open-handedness gives the warmer, more loving atmosphere.

Rules. Keep them few and simple. Two rules are fairly standard: no money handouts, and no "take-out" food. If the guests understand that only food is available and that they need to go to other agencies for financial help, many difficult situations will be avoided. Not allowing food to be carried out reduces neighbors' complaints about litter. Other rules may be needed later, but in the beginning, the fewer the better.

Servers' attitudes toward the people being served are more important than rules. A positive attitude that respects people's dignity is likely to be returned in kind. Volunteers in one Texas soup kitchen refer to all patrons as 'sir' or 'ma'am.' In many kitchens the guests are given an opportunity to volunteer their services by helping with chores like setting up and taking down the tables. This provides them with the chance to claim some ownership and pride instead of being passive "recipients."

Legalities. You will need a tax-exempt status to enable donors to receive a tax deduction. (See chapter 1.) In some states you may also need a special I.D. number to buy from wholesalers without paying sales tax: Ask a local wholesaler how to get one. You must also contact the local board of health and perhaps the fire marshall about their regulations. Consulting a lawyer can be helpful, particularly in deciding whether to incorporate. Check on insurance coverage for liability if a volunteer or a guest should be injured.

Sources of Food. Donations of food and money by individuals and organizations is certainly one major source. (See chapters 18 and 20.) The U.S. Department of Agriculture, through its Food and Nutrition Service, offers surplus commodities such as dairy products, grains and honey to charitable organizations under Public Law 480. Check with your state agriculture commission. Food banks generally sell food for as little as 10 cents per pound. Check with Second Harvest (address in appendix) to find the nearest food bank. Wholesalers, producers, grocery stores, produce markets and day-old-bread stores are often amazingly generous. Many chain stores donate food that has passed its sale date but is still good. Businesses are most likely to give out of enlightened self-interest when they get both a tax deduction and good publicity. Always follow up a donation with a thank-you letter that mentions specifically what has been donated and its approximate monetary value so the donor can get a tax deduction.

Be prompt in picking up whatever is offered, and take all that is offered, or the business may be unwilling to deal with you in the future. If your soup kitchen cannot use all of it, other charitable organizations nearby can. Sharing resources is much more productive than guarding them jealously.

Volunteers. (See chapter 2) Publicity within sponsoring organizations (posters, announcements, church bulletins, newsletters) and to the public (newspapers, etc.) will usually bring plenty of volunteers. Training volunteers is essential. Many have never been exposed to people who have no change of clothing, no way to keep clean, no medical or dental care or who are angry and bitter about their need. This can be hard for the well-meaning volunteer to handle. Most volunteers also

---

SUGGESTED EQUIPMENT (to feed 100)

(The equipment you need will depend on the type of food served.)

2 deep pots (48 qt.)
3 long spoons (wooden ones don't get hot)
2 doz. plastic or wicker baskets (for serving "soup bread" or sandwiches on the tables)
2 coffee urns (80-cup size)
4-6 big plastic buckets with handles for mixing and carrying dry milk
2 large bowls (7 qt. or larger) for mixing sandwich spreads
4-6 spatulas for spreading sandwich fillings
1 food processor (for grinding meats and cheeses for spreads; for chopping vegetables for soup)
2-3 paring knives and vegetable peelers for preparing fresh vegetables
4 large oven pans (12 × 18 × 2)
10-12 pitchers (metal or plastic) for pouring soup and beverages
1 commercial meat slicing machine (used primarily for slicing the 5-lb. blocks of government surplus cheese)
100 plastic soup bowls or divided plates (styrofoam cups work for soup, but are expensive and ecologically unsound)
4 ice cream scoops (1 cup size) for serving casseroles
plenty of trays

need training in dealing with guests who have severe physical or emotional problems. Post emergency phone numbers (police, alcohol treatment center, ambulance) prominently in the kitchen and make sure all volunteers are aware of their location.

Volunteers also need instruction in preparing and serving food, such as whether to use crusts, to use mayonnaise or mustard on one side of the sandwich or both, how many packets of sugar per person, etc. Often new recruits prepare the food while more experienced volunteers serve the guests, but at least one experienced worker should be in the kitchen to answer questions.

Personal contact can raise the volunteers' awareness of the poor as people and provide opportunity for growth in "loving the unloveable." Or it can be a distressing and painful ordeal. Arrange regular volunteer meetings monthly or bi-monthly as a time to discuss problems and attitudes and give one another encouragement and support. A monthly newsletter helps build a sense of community and can be a valuable teaching tool.

Remember, food is the least important thing a soup kitchen provides. More important is dignity, the feeling of community and a loving, accepting atmosphere.

9

Start a Shelter

By Mary Jo Dellinger

S tarting and maintaining a shelter program is rewarding but difficult. Common sense suggests a look at all possible reasons for not getting involved before you begin. A healthy skepticism at first will surface many issues and problems before they become crises. Despite the difficulties many churches, synagogues and other groups have started shelters for homeless people in recent years. The need is great. In Atlanta, for instance, more than 30 voluntary groups provide shelter for up to 2,000 homeless people.

If your congregation is considering a shelter, talk with the pastor or rabbi, who will probably not be involved with running the shelter but whose support will be critical. With a church, a YWCA or any kind of organization you will also need a task group of people committed to the shelter as well as the permission and support of the organization's official governing body. (See chapter 1.)

Setting Up the Shelter

First the group must find a location. Many shelters are located in churches. If you plan to use these facilities, several issues will need to be settled early. Check fire codes and other requirements with the local fire department. One church had to change plans because the required second exit was a few feet too far away. Fire or health department regulations may also affect the number of persons that can be housed on the premises. Find out if shelter meals can be cooked on site or prepared elsewhere and brought in. Whether the shelter will share space with other programs or have its own space will affect decisions about what hours it will operate and what programs can be offered for guests.

If you plan to use a building other than a church you will need to look at zoning issues as well. You will need a building that is suitable, in a convenient location and approved for multi-family housing. One group worked with the Housing Authority in their community to set up a shelter in space provided in a public housing project. Location will determine whether you will serve a walk-in population or will need to provide transportation. If the shelter is not near public transportation you may need a designated place to pick up guests each night and deliver them in the mornings. If the shelter is on a bus route decide whether to provide bus fare for guests. Some shelters do; others give bus fare only to folks who are working and need transportation to and from work until their first paycheck arrives.

Decide what population the shelter will serve. In most cities the greatest number of homeless people are single men, but the numbers of women, children and entire families seeking shelter is growing. The needs and problems of different kinds of homeless people are quite distinct—even conflicting at times—and most shelters find they have to specialize. Some house only men while others house women and children, entire families or women only.

You will also need to set an acceptance policy and decide whether to limit how long guests may stay. Some shelters take people on a first-come, first-served basis until they reach capacity. Others encourage guests to remain for longer periods and accept new people only as previous guests move on. Some set a maximum length of a month or two; others let people stay as long as they wish. Some, particularly those working to counsel people and place them in jobs, insist on a minimum stay and ask guests to commit to the program for two weeks or even six months.

Some shelters are open only when the temperature drops below a certain level or only during the winter while others stay open all year around. Limiting shelter operation to cold weather does save lives and keeps the task more manageable with volunteers and a small budget. Problems of homeless people, however, extend far beyond surviving the cold, and the shelter that remains open all year will be able to provide more comprehensive help.

Finally, decide whether to depend entirely on volunteers or have one or more paid staff. Most of the volunteers in shelters run by churches and synagogues come from within the congregation and from other congregations in the same neighborhood or same denomination. When looking for volunteers, identify those who might become trainers, working regularly in the shelter and helping train new volunteers once or twice a week. Consistency is important to volunteers and to guests. A core group serves as a regular point of contact for guests and volunteers.

Day-to-Day Operation

Once basic decisions have been made, plan for the day-to-day operation of the shelter. Study the available space. The best layout to use depends on the population the shelter will serve. One year-round shelter houses 12 women in two bedrooms with six women in each room. They began six years ago with mattresses on the floor but now have a bed and bedside table for each guest. Another, for men, sleeps a dozen in three rooms with two bunk beds in each room. A family shelter in a synagogue has a separate room for each family. A large downtown church houses 50 men on mats on the gym floor. You will need to balance the desire to help as many people as possible against the privacy and individual support that can be offered to a smaller number.

Decide whether to allow guests to leave personal belongings at the shelter during the day. Having a secure place to keep things can be vitally important to someone living on the street, but without any kind of policy the accumulated belongings can take over the shelter space. Some shelters provide lockers; others let guests store belongings under their beds.

A bath and clean clothes boost the morale of someone out on the streets all day, so offer shower and laundry facilities to your guests if you can. If they are not already in place, decide if you can offer them and find out about installation. Showers don't take much space. One shelter removed a toilet stall in the rest room to install a shower and replaced a sink with a washer and a dryer. If you provide sheets and towels, a washer and dryer are essential. Some smaller shelters allow each guest a certain night to do laundry. In others, volunteers wash a couple of loads for guests each night. Some launder sheets and towels during the day so the machines will be available for guests in the evening.

Next, look at kitchen facilities and decide about meals. Generally, your needs, options and problems will be the same as for running a soup kitchen. (See chapter 8.) Some smaller shelters keep bread, cereals, milk, coffee or tea for breakfast. They have a refrigerator and a microwave and use disposable utensils. Food volunteers bring an evening meal they have prepared at home. Churches that have a regular meal on Wednesday or Sunday evenings often include shelter guests in those meals—a good way for guests and members of the congregation to get to know each other and to involve more church members in the ministry.

Volunteers

Volunteers are key to the success of a shelter ministry. (See chapter 2 on nurturing volunteers.) Based on the experience of many shelters it takes 50 to 60 committed volunteers to run a small shelter (fewer than 20 guests) without serious risk of burnout. Every shelter needs regular ways to recruit and train additional volunteers since some will be lost through normal attrition.

Many shelters assign two volunteers for duty each night. Normally one person could handle the responsibility, but two are wise in case of emergency. Some shelters ask volunteers to come when the shelters open in the evening and stay until guests leave the next morning. Others ask volunteers to work in shifts. The first shift comes early to prepare the evening meal; the second comes in at nine or ten and spends the night; the third comes in the morning to take care of breakfast and cleanup. What will work best for you depends on the nature of your shelter and the volunteers' schedules.

Volunteers' schedules depend on your circumstances. Some shelters assign each participating congregation or organization responsibility for finding volunteers for one week a month: Others ask each volunteer for a six-month commitment and provide a calendar that notes the nights assigned according to each person's request. One volunteer reminds people of their assigned night and fills empty slots with new volunteers.

Job descriptions for volunteers are helpful in recruiting. Don't limit recruiting to those people who are actually available during the hours the shelter operates. You will also need people who can call others to remind them of shelter commitments, to set up calendars, to help with recruitment and with public programs and to raise money.

Recruit through notices in church bulletins and organizational newsletters, but don't expect written notices to solve the continuing need for volunteers. Most people get involved because someone they know asks them to help. Encourage every volunteer to become a volunteer recruiter. Suggest they first bring a friend or co-worker to the shelter with them so they can become acquainted with the program before committing themselves.

Several shelter committees publish volunteer handbooks, outlining the purpose of the shelter ministry, tasks which need to be done, duties of volunteers, rules for guests, suggested menus and emergency numbers. Each volunteer receives a copy.

Funding

Determine how money will need to be raised for both start up and regular operating expenses. (See chapter 3 for ideas on fundraising.) Often a church or synagogue will provide the space and utilities, and many also include the cost of the shelter's operation in their annual budget. Sometimes a partnership of several congregations may take on the responsibilities of funding and providing volunteers. Some shelters collect donations from individuals or grants from foundations or the government, particularly for start-up costs and renovation. Sunday school classes or youth groups sometimes adopt a shelter and provide regular funding, appliances or labor to paint and fix up the shelter area.

Don't forget business contacts when you look at the shelter's needs. Ask for donations or discounts on mattresses, cots, sheets, appliances, etc. If people know precisely what you need and are asked directly, many will respond positively.

Special Problems

Many groups are reluctant to begin a shelter because they fear it will be depressing or even dangerous. A few simple rules will prevent most serious problems, and good training for volunteers can give them the confidence and skill to deal with those that come up.

Most shelters strictly prohibit alcohol and drugs and refuse to admit guests who are obviously intoxicated. Requiring guests to stay until the next morning, once they've been admitted to the shelter, can also cut down on alcohol and drug problems. Those shelters that house the same people for longer periods of time generally also have policies that allow them to suspend a guest's stay for repeated drunkenness, starting fights or other major infractions. Have pastors, counselors or social workers on call for serious situations.

Be sure to visit other shelters and talk with volunteers. Take advantage of their expertise; ask what has worked and not worked for them. Get copies of their rules and guidelines. Continue meeting with them after your shelter is operating. If you don't know who runs shelters in your community, ask the Salvation Army, the church council or ministerial alliance, United Way or a local HELP line.

To let homeless people know about your shelter, contact soup kitchens, day labor pools, day shelters and other night shelters about two weeks before you open. Let them know when you will open, the hours of operations and the number of and type of people to be served. Ask them to refer people to you. Don't be discouraged if only a few people show up the first night. If your shelter meets a real need in the community, it will fill up within a few weeks as the word spreads.

Expect that some policies and procedures carefully worked out in advance will not work. Be flexible and learn from mistakes, from shelter guests and from people working in other shelters. The longer you work with homeless people the more you will want to do and the more opportunities you will find. One final word of caution: *Do only what you can do well.* Don't take on so much that volunteers and staff become overextended and ineffective. Continue to involve new people and thus, spread the concern and increase the ability to help.

10

Volunteer Overseas

By Jan Buckingham

I f you would like to volunteer, the first place to look is at yourself. List your skills, interests, abilities, special areas of expertise and what languages you speak. Decide if there are places you will not go and things you don't want to do. Write down exactly why you want to volunteer.

To make it as a volunteer you need to be flexible, independent and committed to helping others. You also need a sense of humor. Add to that, interdependence in relationships with the ability to give and take.

It's okay to be idealistic; that's probably why you're thinking of volunteering. But if your plan is to save the world, one village or even your neighborhood, watch out. At best, you can be a part of the solution, an agent for change. But as a short-term or even a long-term volunteer, you can hardly expect to reverse decades of poverty, inequality, racism or pain.

Volunteering can be very satisfying. President Jimmy Carter who volunteers with Habitat for Humanity said, "Active participation in a worthy project can bring great pleasure, gratification and benefit— most often more rewarding to the volunteer than to those we are attempting to help. There should always be an element of sharing, of partnership—not an attitude of superiority or self-congratulation."

Finding a place to volunteer isn't hard, but finding one that suits you and one where you suit the challenge may take some time. Look for a group that meets your expectations about volunteer service. There should be enough travel compensation, stipends and other benefits for you to manage. The position should fit your skills and availability and suit you physically, spiritually and philosophically. When you have finished your personal inventory, it is time to look at lists of volunteer organizations.

The following list is by no means exhaustive, and omission from this list should not be read as a negative comment.

American Friends Service Committee

1501 Cherry Street, Philadelphia, PA 19102, (215) 241-7000
This Quaker organization accepts interdenominational volunteers to re-

pair schools, clinics, roads, houses and irrigation systems. They also work with reforestation, gardening and health and nutrition concerns. A $500 fee is required (scholarships available). **Area served:** Mexico. **Volunteer needs:** Construction workers, gardeners and child-care assistants. **Number needed:** 100. **Length of service:** 6-8 weeks. **Prerequisites:** 18-26 years of age; Spanish. **Benefits:** Housing, food, insurance.

Brethren Volunteer Service
1451 Dundee Ave., Elgin, IL 60120, (312) 742-5100
Church of the Brethren seeks interdenominational volunteers for community services, health care, agricultural assistance, housing and work with senior citizens. They will address peace and hunger issues and domestic violence. Older people as well as young adults are encouraged to apply. Service begins with a three-week orientation. **Area served:** 20 U.S. states and 15 foreign countries. **Volunteers needed:** Social workers, teachers, office workers, gardeners, community organizers, English teachers, construction workers, youth workers and child-care workers. **Number needed:** 125. **Length of service:** U.S., one year; foreign, two years. **Prerequisites:** 18 years old. **Benefits:** Housing, food, insurance, stipend of $35 a month first year and $45 second year.

Christian Reformed World Relief
2850 Kalamazoo Ave., S.E., Grand Rapids, MI 49560,(616) 246-0738
Christian, interdenominational volunteers sought for disaster relief, long-term recovery response and community services. Preference given to denomination members and volunteers aged 55-75. **Areas served:** U.S. **Volunteers needed:** Volunteers with administrative, advocacy, construction, plumbing, carpentry, bricklaying, electrical, drywall skills. **Number needed:** 30. **Benefits:** Housing, food, workmen's compensation insurance.

Concern
P.O. Box 1790, Santa Ana, CA 92702, (714)953-8575
This interdenominational organization needs doctors, nurses, midwives and agriculturalists for training and education. They will also work in nutrition rehabilitation centers and do sanitation development. A medical clinic is planned for Tiajuana. **Area served:** Bangladesh, El Salvador, Mexico, Sierra Leone, Honduras, Nigeria and Sudan. **Number needed:** 125. **Length of service:** One year minimum. **Prerequisites:** Degree in public health, nutrition, agriculture, engineering, medicine, Spanish in Latin America. **Benefits:** $50 monthly stipend, $50/month readjustment allowance after completion of service, housing, food, transportation, insurance.

Direct Relief International
P.O. Box 30820, Santa Barbara, CA 93130, (805) 687-3694
DRI provides a nonsectarian, nonpolitical volunteer medical services program to developing nations. They seek to strengthen the health base

by supplying medical services (and supplies) to indigenous hospitals. Married couples are welcome to apply. **Areas served:** U.S., Africa, Asia, Latin America, the Pacific and the Caribbean. **Volunteers needed:** GP's, nurses, dentists, pediatricians, specialists. Number needed: 100-150. **Length of service:** Short- and long-term. **Prerequisites:** Medical professional, varied language requirements. **Benefits:** Housing, food.

Franciscan Volunteer Community

109 N. Dearborn, Suite 404, Chicago, IL 60602, 312-532-2333
The Chicago Parish Ministry is active in shelters and soup kitchens and will soon be opening a new soup kitchen. Catholic volunteers are preferred. Chicago. **Volunteers needed:** Willing committed Christians. **Number needed:** 15. **Length of service:** U.S.: one year; will accept students for short term. **Prerequisites:** Prefer high school graduate at least 20 years old. **Benefits:** Stipend, room, food.

Habitat for Humanity

Habitat and Church Streets, Americus, GA 31709, (912) 924-6935
Habitat, a Christian, interdenominational organization, builds and renovates homes for the inadequately sheltered. It was formed in 1976 as an outgrowth of Koinonia Partners and offers no-interest mortgages payable over a 15-25 year period. **Areas served:** Over 200 locations in North America; in 40 countries around the world; headquarters in Americus, GA. **Volunteers needed:** Accountants, bookkeepers, clerical and office workers, construction workers and people in public relations, word processing, graphic arts, photography skills. **Number needed:** 225. **Length of service:** Short-term projects vary; long-term projects one month to three years in U.S.; three years overseas. **Prerequisites:** None, but construction and administrative skills are encouraged. Language instruction provided. **Benefits:** U.S.: housing and food stipend; Overseas: $300/month individuals, $500/month couples (plus $150/child).

Health Volunteers Overseas, Inc.

c/o Washington Station, P.O. Box 65157, Washington, D.C. 20035-5157, (202) 296-0928
HVO is dedicated to voluntary assistance for the advancement of health training and care in developing countries. Rather than service they emphasize teaching in basic medical care with available, affordable and appropriate equipment. **Area served:** Central and South America, Africa and Asia. **Volunteers needed:** Orthopedic surgeons, anesthesiologists, general surgeons, oral and maxillofacial surgeons, physical therapists, nurses. **Number needed:** 60. **Length of service:** one month. **Prerequisites:** Medical or health degree. **Benefits:** In most cases transportation and lodging paid by volunteer.

Heifer Project International

P.O. Box 808, Little Rock, AR 72203, (501) 376-6836
In partnership with low-income farmers, this interdenominational organization supplies livestock and technical assistance. There are con-

ference facilities on a 1,200 acre ranch for development and technical education. Animals at the center include Brangus cattle, donkeys, draft horses, sheep, goats, pigs, chickens, rabbits, bees and fish. If you've never worked with animals, you will be trained. Internships available for college credit. **Areas served:** International Learning Livestock Center in Arkansas, with active projects in 11 U.S. states and 40 foreign countries. **Volunteers needed:** General farm/livestock workers; construction workers; hospitality, cafeteria, cleaning, office work; educators; media volunteers; and speakers. **Prerequisites:** Must be at least 18 years old. **Length of service:** Varies, usually short-term. **Benefits:** Small stipend, food, housing, accident insurance.

International Voluntary Service, Inc.

1424-16th St., N.W., Suite 204, Washington, D.C., 20016, (202) 387-5533
IVS promotes grassroots development by offering technical assistance volunteers to the third world. They assist in agriculture, health training, small business, forestry and medicine. Volunteers must be comfortable with informal teaching atmosphere. **Areas served:** Africa, South America, Central America, Eastern Caribbean. **Volunteers needed:** Veterinarians, livestock specialists, mechanical engineers, management accountants, agricultural training. **Number needed:** 50. **Length of service:** 2-3 years. **Prerequisites:** Graduate degree, two years previous third world work experience, Spanish for Central America programs; instruction provided for other placements. **Benefits:** Cost of living allowance (varies), $200/month vacation allowance, housing, transportation, education for children.

Jesuit Volunteer Corps

P.O. Box 32692, Detroit, MI 48232, (313) 894-1140
This Catholic organization aids the aged, the homeless and the handicapped, working in shelters and soup kitchens. They emphasize a simple lifestyle, social justice and Christian community. Volunteers work in both rural and urban areas. **Area served:** Throughout the U.S. **Volunteers needed:** Teachers, youth ministry workers, drop-in workers, health care specialists, nurses, battered women's advocates, community organizers. **Number needed:** 300. **Prerequisites:** College degree or work experience. Spanish for some Southern and Southeastern placements. **Length of service:** one year. Benefits: Stipend, housing, food, health insurance, transportation.

Lutheran Volunteer Corps

1333 N. St., N.W., Washington, D.C., 20005, (202) 387-3222
This group is interdenominational and encourages "intentional Christian communities." The Corps works with shelters for the homeless, senior citizens and youth, community organizing, policy and advocacy work (hunger and peace issues), and other social justice-related work. No specific skills are required and agencies and their needs vary from year to year. **Areas served:** Baltimore, Chicago, Milwaukee, Washington, D.C., Wilmington. **Number needed:** 40-50. **Length of service:** one

year, may be renewed. **Prerequisites:** Must be at least 21 years of age. No upper age limit. No language requirement except certain agencies that require Spanish. **Benefits:** $85/month stipend, housing and food, health insurance, transportation.

Maryknoll Lay Missioners

Maryknoll, NY 10545, (914) 762-6364
As a branch of the Catholic Foreign Mission Society of America, "We respond to the needs of the poor and oppressed." The projects include pastoral work, medical assistance, health education, teaching, agriculture extension, community development and communication. **Areas served:** Africa, Central America, South America, Philippines, Japan, Korea. **Volunteers needed:** Agronomists, volunteers with audio-visual or TV experience. **Number needed:** 125. **Length of service:** 3½ years, following a four-month orientation. **Prerequisites:** Must be U.S. Catholic with college degree or skill followed by a minimum of one-year's experience; generally, must be 23-40 years old. Language instruction provided. **Benefits:** $150/month stipend, monthly living allowance, vacation allowance, housing, transportation, medical insurance, reimbursement of $400/year.

Mennonite Central Committee

21 South 12th Street, Akron, PA 17501, (717) 859-1151
MCC is the service and relief agency of the Mennonite and Brethren in Christ Churches in the U.S and Canada. They respond with a Christian, non-violent approach to work in education, agriculture and nutrition, economic and technical development, justice advocacy and research. **Areas served:** 50 countries, including the U.S. and Canada. **Volunteers needed:** Agriculturalists, water development specialists, science and math teachers, public and community health specialists. **Number needed:** 950-1,000. **Length of service:** U.S., 2 years; Overseas, 3 years. **Prerequisites:** Church-member, dedicated to non-violence. Language instruction provided. **Benefits:** $43/month for adults ($25/child); housing, food, round-trip transportation, medical care, vacation allowance, children's education.

Peace Corps

806 Connecticut Ave. N.W., Suite M-1214, Washington, D.C. 20526, (800) 424-8580, ext. 93
Since 1961 over 115,000 have served in projects that help promote progress through self-help emphasizing mutual world peace and mutual understanding between the U.S. and people of developing nations. Peace Corps volunteers have worked with maternal and child health, nutrition, fresh-water fisheries, agriculture extension, teacher training, small business development, forestry, conservation and energy. Apply six to nine months, but no more than a year, in advance. If married, must serve with spouse; couples with children not encouraged. Disabled persons welcome to apply. **Areas served:** 60 nations in Latin America, Africa, Asia and the Pacific. **Volunteers needed:** Specialists in agriculture,

forestry, nursing, engineering, industrial arts, home economics, special education, science and math education, public health, occupational therapy, accounting. **Number needed:** 5,300. Actively recruiting older Americans and minorities; 11% of all volunteers today are over 50. **Length of service:** 2 years, following 3 months of training. **Prerequisites:** Bachelor's degree or 3-5 years experience in needed vocation. Language instruction provided. **Benefits:** $100-200/living allowance, plus a $175/month readjustment allowance for every month of service following completion of program; immunizations, health services provided.

Presbyterian Church (USA) Volunteers in Mission

475 Riverside Dr., Room 1126, New York, NY 10115, (212) 870-2802
Typical projects are medical service (doctor, nurse and specialist placement, hospital administration), education, community advocacy (hunger and peace issues). VIM helps church-related organizations find full-time volunteers. Most volunteers are college age, post-college young adults or retired persons. **Areas served:** U.S. and overseas. **Volunteers needed:** Doctors, nurses, teachers, community organizers, social workers, youth workers. **Number needed:** U.S., 300; overseas, 100. **Prerequisites:** Church-member. Language requirements vary (instruction provided for some). **Length of service:** U.S.: 3-24 months; overseas: 2-4 years. **Benefits:** Housing, food, transportation.

Southern Baptist Foreign Mission Board

Volunteers in Missions, P.O. Box 6767, Richmond, VA 23230, (804) 353-0151
Volunteers in Missions combines evangelism with meeting needs. Volunteers must be willing to go at a time specified by field missionary. Currently, volunteers are working in over 50 countries on projects of general health care, well digging, construction, disaster relief, education, ESL placement overseas. **Areas served:** Latin America, Africa, Asia, Oceania. **Volunteers needed:** Specialized needs based on requests from the field. **Number needed:** For human needs: 2,000. **Length of service:** Two weeks to two years. **Prerequisites:** Active member of Southern Baptist Church with pastor's recommendation, vital Christian testimony, good health and skills. **Benefits:** Volunteers furnish own living and transportation expenses. Some assistance provided for one- and two-year assignments.

VISTA

c/o ACTION, Washington, D.C. 20525. (202) 634-9445
VISTA is designed to strengthen and supplement efforts to eliminate poverty and poverty-related human, social and environmental problems in the U.S. They provide economic development assistance and neighborhood revitalization. They work with food banks, literacy programs, job training, youth education about drug use and child abuse. Volunteers live and work among the poor in urban and rural areas, including Indian reservations. Focuses on the mobilization of community resources. Over one-third of volunteers are from low-income backgrounds. **Area served:** All over U.S. **Volunteers needed:** Specialized needs based on requests

from the sponsor organization. **Number needed:** 2,400. **Prerequisites:** Age 18 and older. Generally no language requirements although some projects require bilingual volunteers. **Length of service:** 1 year. **Benefits:** Subsistence allowance, $75/month readjustment allowance at end of service, housing, vacation allowance, medical insurance.

Volunteer Missionary Movement

8901 S. Hamilton Ave., Chicago, IL 60620, (312) 233-9440
Founded in 1969 in England and established in USA in 1981, VMM is a lay movement within the Catholic Church with ecumenical membership that shares skills in mission with the overseas Church. Education, medicine, technology development, pastoral work. VMM aims to tackle poverty, disease and illiteracy. Program includes a one-week introduction course in Illinois and a 5-week preparation course in London. **Area served:** Africa, Papua New Guinea. **Volunteers needed:** Secondary school teachers, doctors, nurses, midwives, carpenters, mechanics, agriculturalists, administrators. Number needed: 100-120. **Length of service:** 2 years with option to renew. **Prerequisites:** Professional skill, one-year's work experience, practicing Christian. Language instruction provided. **Benefits:** Monthly stipend, housing.

Volunteers in Overseas Cooperative Assistance (VOCA)

50 F Street, N.W., Suite 900, Washington, D.C. 20001, (202)628-0066
VOCA provides short-term technical assistance to cooperatives, farm associations and government agencies in developing countries. Typical projects are agriculture marketing, helping establish credit unions, housing assistance, rural electric, rural telephone and assistance/advice to farm associations. The organization receives funding from its member organizations, from supporters and from U.S.A.I.D. **Area served:** Over 30 developing countries. **Number of volunteers needed:** 100-200 per year. **Length of service:** Up to 90 days. **Prerequisites:** Must be a retired or senior level cooperative executive or successful U.S. farmer. Foreign language desirable but interpreter provided. **Benefits:** Housing, food, transportation, clothing care.

Volunteers in Technical Assistance (VITA) *1815 N. Lynn Street, Suite 200, Arlington, VA 22209, (703)276-1800*

VITA works on small and medium scale technical assistance projects. It is generally an information service for people in the third world. Questions addressed to VITA are answered through correspondence by in-house staff first. If further information is needed a data base of volunteers is consulted. Inquiries and follow-up are done by correspondence. Sometimes staff or volunteers are sent to work on a project. **Area served:** The third world. **Volunteers needed:** 40 on staff, 12 overseas and 5,000 volunteer consultants on the data base. **Length of service:** On demand. **Prerequisites:** Availability and technical expertise. **Benefits:** Volunteers on data-base get monthly news letter and those contacted for work abroad get varied compensation. Staff is salaried with benefits.

World Concern

P.O. Box 33000, Seattle, WA 98133, (206)546-7201
This interdenominational organization, that is always in partnership and second to the indigenous agency, provides technical assistance in rural food and development projects. They focus on food production, veterinary and animal husbandry, water development and primary health care. **Areas served:** South Asia, South East Asia, Haiti, Bolivia, East Africa. **Volunteers needed:** Health workers, teachers in non-institutional setting, social workers for refugee work in S.E. Asia, agronomists, veterinarians, extension workers. **Number needed:** 45. **Length of service:** 2-3 years. **Prerequisites:** Degree and/or experience. Motivation to work cross-culturally and out of a Christain faith. Those not speaking the native language will attend language school. **Benefits:** Modest salary, housing, transportation for the volunteers and their families. Schooling cost for families with children, health insurance.

World Relief Corporation

P.O. Box WRC, Wheaton, IL 60189, (312) 665-0235
World Relief, interdenominational and a member of the National Association of Evangelicals, was founded in 1944 to help the "poorest of the poor" and to restore their "dignity and self-respect." Typical projects are community development, refugee programs and disaster relief. Projects include agriculture, water, medical, education, nursing, income generation, women in development and others.**Area served:** Africa, Central America, Asia and U.S. **Volunteers needed:** English as a second language (ESL) teachers for refugee programs. Other needs vary according to project. **Number needed:** 30-35. **Length of service:** 1 year minimum. **Prerequisites:** Experience, college degree preferred. Language requirements vary. **Benefits:** Vary but usually include monthly stipend, housing, food, insurance.

World Vision

919 W. Huntington Dr., Monrovia, CA 91016, (818) 357-7979
World Vision promotes world peace and progress through self-help projects and mutual understanding between the U.S. and people of developing nations. Typical projects of this interdenominational organization are distribution of food, medical assistance and community development. World Vision uses qualified professionals to reach out and meet the physical and spiritual needs of the poor throughout the world. **Areas served:** Over 80 countries plus U.S. **Volunteers needed:** Nutritionists, doctors and nurses serving in community health programs, agronomists, logisticians, mechanics, administrators, accountants. **Number needed:** 150. **Length of service:** 1 year minimum. **Prerequisites:** Third world experience. Language requirements vary, French, Portuguese. **Benefits:** Stipend, housing, food, transportation.

Reach Out to a Sister City

By Gary Gunderson

I n his landmark book, *Small Is Beautiful,* E.F. Schumacher described global hunger as a problem of two million villages with distinct opportunities, liabilities, skills, resources and hopes. Our response to world hunger must also make sense at the village level or not at all.

Through Sister Cities International, more than 750 communities in the United States and Europe are building direct, people-to-people links with villages throughout the poorer nations of the world. About 25 of these cooperatively attack problems of water, sanitation, health, education and nutrition.

Baltimore, Maryland, and, Gbarnga, Liberia, have been linked for over a decade. The relationship began with a recognition of historic slave ties and with donations of clothing and supplies. But over the years many people traveled back and forth, and the Baltimore committee came to understand the vital contribution the Liberians could make to the educational system in Baltimore. The Liberians helped design a new curriculum that introduced African culture and history and brought an important subject alive in a new way.

Sister city relationships have also been formed through the Partners of the Americas program or as an independent community initiative. The committees from both communities draw upon and supplement the work of churches, civic groups, international organizations, schools and professional associations.

The following steps can help you form a sister city relationship in your community.

Step One: Get the emphasis right.

People, not money or resources, link communities. The structure channels energy, mutual assistance and even economic benefits through the power of human relationship. This makes the project unpredictable. What begins as a response to world hunger may result in building a school or seeing your own community's hunger.

Step Two: Look around.

Most U.S. communities are already linked in some way to a village or city in the third world. Over 700 U.S. communities have formal sister city relationships with other communities around the world. A Rotary Club, YMCA, church, university or any organization with international affiliates can provide the burning embers of a relationship that can be fanned into flame. Find those already working internationally and talk with them. Ask the mayor's office, newspaper editor, association of churches, civic clubs, schools and universities. Also talk with international students, former missionaries and overseas businessmen. Keep notes of your conversations, including succinct quotes. You will be surprised at how many people are already interested in the idea of long-term relationships with other communities.

Step Three: Call a meeting of interested people.

The purpose of the first meeting is to discuss formation of an enduring relationship with a third world community. You may meet in your home, the home of a prominent community leader, a church, a bank, the library, the city hall or a newspaper office. Set the meeting at least a month in advance, and let local news media know about it. (See chapter 24 on working with media.) Write a short, informative letter, sharing information from your preliminary conversations and pointing out the most interesting overseas links with specific communities. Mail the letter with a notice about the meeting. You don't need a logo, letterhead and board of directors at this point. People will likely be surprised by and interested in the size and variety of international interests you've unearthed.

Step Four: Decide on an organizational structure.

The sister city relationship is a bit like a marriage. It starts with a little romance and excitement, but needs a responsible legal and financial structure to sustain itself. Most folks don't bring an attorney on their first date. You may not expect to create a formal sister city program, but a structure that has been developed over three decades deserves a close look early in your planning process. Sister Cities International (SCI) exists to help communities like yours link up with communities abroad. Most official sister city committees are legally incorporated, and SCI strongly suggests incorporation for tax exempt status. The point of linking communities is long-term relationship, not a one-shot project. Settling legal issues early allows for long-range planning and stability, and also clearly communicates the style of the relationship. (See chapter 1 on starting a group.)

Alternate Step Four: Work with an existing committee.

Hundreds of communities have existing sister city committees, although only a handful are linked with towns in the developing world. Meet with the committee to see if they are open to forming another relationship with a new sister city. Sister Cities International will help if you ask. Never duplicate an existing organization unless it is fatally flawed.

Step Five: Choose a partner.

Pick a city. Seriously consider several possible communities that present different opportunities. The group must decide which will make the best match and how the relationship can be *mutually* beneficial. The other city probably has much to gain from the health and development projects you'll undertake, but how will *your* community be enriched? Many possibilities will exist if you consider carefully. Local schools can find material for new curricula. Universities could benefit from faculty and student exchanges as well as new programs. The Chamber of Commerce can create international links. Churches may use this effort to undergird their overseas missions emphasis, and Rotary Clubs can exchange members. Even travel agencies may be intrigued. A relationship without mutual benefits is likely to degenerate into a short-lived paternalistic spasm.

Other considerations.

The city should be close enough for regular contact. If the host government is friendly, its embassy in the United States can give help and advice. Decide how to deal with the language barrier. Choose a city whose priorities match your community's and whose local leadership is trustworthy. (Don't be embarrassed to ask—they need to know that about you too.) The U.S. embassy can be a big help if the political context permits. If you want to establish a relationship with a country our government does not consider an ally, ask for and expect to receive the cooperation of our embassy there anyway. Embassy staff are generally career professionals and public servants who want to be helpful to you and to the country in which they are stationed.

Beware of questioning the relationship to death before it has had a chance to blossom. At some point make a choice and stick with it.

Step Six: Go and see.

A small group of sensitive people representing a cross-section from your community must make the first visit. Ask the Mayor to go or to endorse the visit by an official letter. Contact all appropriate officials, especially those in any institution you hope to involve. Don't just wander in as tourists! This may be the first step of a significant, long term relationship and should be treated seriously. Get good, current advice on the situation in the country and how to act. Ask people who've traveled there recently on business, on a student exchange or with the Peace Corps. (The organization of Returned Peace Corps Volunteers keeps a directory and is listed in the index.) A political science teacher who specializes in that area of the world may be helpful.

Step Seven: Spread the word.

Let the local media know when your group goes overseas and invite them to schedule interviews when they return. Chances are, you'll have an engagement to announce. Visitors should be good communicators. They will quickly find their evenings busy with slide shows and speaking engagements. These can simply be first-hand stories with names and vivid experiences rather than highly professional productions.

Step Eight: Cooperate on joint projects.

Don't assume you know what your partner community's needs are just because your community seems less needy. Sometimes the American city is surprised to find itself on the learning end of the friendship. Reston, Virginia, and Nyere, Kenya, came together with a special interest in improving the situation of handicapped people. The Kenyan strategy, which emphasized training the handicapped for economic self-sufficiency, turned out to be highly useful in Virginia.

The best projects will draw on the human resources of both communities. Health care, education, training, sanitation, city planning, water development and construction all offer a chance for personal involvement between the communities. Don't begin any project in either city unless it is initiated by the host committee and is a clear priority for both communities. Be prepared for some frustration: "Obviously, they need a dam more than an elementary school!" On the other side: "Why can't these pampered Americans see that we know our needs more than they can ever understand? Give us the funds and get out of the way!"

Step Nine: Figure out how to pay for it.

Some aspects of friendship are priceless. Others come with invoices. Three types of expenses quickly emerge: travel, ongoing organization and special joint projects. Each appeals to different interests and offers different possibilities for funding.

The easiest to fund by far are joint projects like a well, a school or a scholarship. The second easiest are the modest ongoing expenses. Most can be absorbed by participating organizations, in-kind gifts or membership dues. Occasional larger gifts may show up to strengthen the catalytic role of the local committee once the relationship is established and producing visible results.

The trickiest cost is often travel, especially in the early stages. Individuals unavoidably carry most of this burden. But travel doesn't have to be restricted to the rich. For key people without means, ask for help from churches, businesses, travel agents and civic organizations. A letter of support and explanation from the local committee will help. Think of the fundraising as a chance to broaden involvement in the project. A church or civic club which financially supports the journey of one of its members has an increased interest in the outcome. If the sister city relationship is formalized, travel agreed upon by both communities may be underwritten by Sister Cities International. Other international organizations such as Partners of the Americas and Rotary International also have travel scholarships.

Explore ways to help your counterpart committee travel to your city. Ask the U.S. embassy for help getting key people to your community. In most countries they offer travel scholarships for key academics and local leaders to come to this country. Also, let the sister city's embassy in this country know of your interest in hosting visitors and arranging speaking events. You may be surprised by their cooperation. Make use of visitors traveling in the United States on other business.

Step Ten: Broaden the ownership.

Never speak without giving members of the audience ways to participate. Get the names and addresses of everyone who wants to be kept informed. Ask for funds or donated material if appropriate. Maybe you'll need homes for visitors or people who speak Spanish or Chinese and who can translate letters. Keep looking for creative, practical ways to involve more people and organizations and broaden the ownership of the project. Unlike a marriage, this relationship gets stronger the more people that are involved.

Finally, stay flexible.

If the relationship is alive, it will be unpredictable. Don't smother it in your preconceived blueprint. Keep your eyes open for the ripple effects of a lively, international partnership. Keep the press informed. You'll notice articles on Africa, for instance, getting into print that weren't there before because the newspaper editor knows your city is linked to one there. Keep your Congressional representatives abreast of your involvement. Let them know how their votes affect not just *your* city, but your sister city. Make sure they understand that their vote for foreign aid means fewer sick children in your counterpart community, for instance.

As the relationships develop, the suffering of hungry people will stop being anonymous and abstract. You'll know people by name and hear their voices not merely speaking of a desperate present but beckoning you to share a future that is better for the joining.

Part Three

Work For Justice

We the people of the United States, in order to form a more perfect Union, establish justice, insure domestic tranquility, provide for the common defense, promote the general welfare, and secure the blessings of liberty to ourselves and our posterity, do ordain and establish this constitution for the United States of America.

—Preamble to the U.S. Constitution

Unfortunately, words alone cannot establish justice, insure domestic tranquility or promote the general welfare. Words alone don't put food on the table or find a job for someone who's unemployed. If we expect our government to do these things, we need to work to make them happen. This work is called advocacy.

The chapters that follow will help us advocate for the poor and hungry in ways that bring results. Issues can change from year to year and from state to state. Promoting the general welfare can mean calling on Congress to provide more money for Women, Infants and Children (WIC), the program that supplies nutritional food for poor children and pregnant or nursing women, or calling on state legislatures to insist on subsidized breakfasts for poor children, or calling on the local food stamp office to remove the barriers that keep eligible people from applying.

Justice can mean advocating for micro-loans by the Agency for International Development to help poor people in third world countries become self-sufficient. It can mean insisting that our city governments reserve a portion of contracts for buildings and roads for firms headed by minorities and women: those who have historically been denied those opportunities.

Obviously, getting the government to act is not the only way to help hungry people. Emergency care such as soup kitchens, night shelters and food pantries in some cases go beyond what the government can do. Volunteers motivated by compassion can reach out in ways not possible for a harried government case worker. On the other hand, governments can do things beyond the capacity of private, voluntary groups. Our voluntary emergency service networks, compassionate and efficient as they are, cannot keep up with the growing need for help. After all, we establish governments to do jobs beyond the scope of private groups. As citizens we can ensure that they do that job.

12

Influence Public Policy Through Congress

From Oxfam America

Attempts to publicize the famine in Ethiopia went unheeded until October 25, 1984—the day of an NBC news broadcast. The overwhelming response of the American public helped lead the U.S. government to provide urgently needed food assistance. Until then, the government had done little.

A decision by TransAfrica to picket the South African Embassy in Washington, D.C., led to a dramatic change in the Free South Africa Movement in the United States. Daily pickets at South African consulates soon caught on around the country. Celebrities, grassroots organizations, and concerned citizens demanded changes in U.S. government policy toward South Africa. Students and faculty at U.S. colleges and universities also stepped up pressure for divestment of stocks in companies doing business in South Africa.

Individuals and groups need to take a stand for justice here and abroad. If you're not a celebrity or the issue isn't as straightforward as famine relief, you can still have an impact. Here are some suggestions.

Letter Writing

Writing letters to Congress can be an important tool for shaping legislation. Congress, however, receives more than 500,000 pieces of mail a day—that's about 935 letters for every legislator. To make your letter stand out, remember these points:

Be timely. Right after a bill has been introduced is the time to ask your representative to co-sponsor the bill, offer amendments or vote a particular way.

Be positive and constructive. If possible, begin your opening sentence by thanking them for a previous vote, speech or position. Clip articles from your newspaper or representative's newsletter for future reference.

Keep the letter short and concise. Don't make a laundry list of recommendations. Be specific: Cite the bill number or title, your position and what you want, such as their co-sponsoring a bill or voting a particular way.

Avoid form letters. Letters should reflect your own ideas and experiences. Typed or neatly handwritten letters are best.

Follow up. If the response from your representative is inadequate or does not answer your concerns, write another letter asking for more specific information.

Say thanks. Many groups write numerous letters advocating their positions without ever sending a simple note of thanks after the vote. Also remember to thank legislators who are often on your side.

Example of an Effective Lobby Letter

> 3090 South 2700 East
> Salt Lake City, UT 84109
> May 19, 1982

The Honorable Orrin Hatch
United States Senate
Washington, D.C. 20510

Dear Senator Hatch:

As a member of NETWORK, a Catholic social-justice lobby, I am concerned about the passage of the Voting Rights Extension Act (S1992).

Although you voted against the Dole-Kennedy-Mathias compromise version of the Voting Rights Act Extension Bill in committee, I urge you to vote for the bill when it comes before the full Senate. I understand your reservations about the "effects test" in earlier versions of the bill; surely this compromise version takes care to prevent the potential problems you expressed concern about in your appearances on television news. I cannot see how the bill could be effective with only the "intent test." Intent to discriminate seems impossible to prove.

Because of the number of instances in which the voting rights of minority citizens have been violated in all parts of this country, I feel it is imperative that the extension be passed.

> Sincerely,
>
> Margaret Orleans

Telephoning

Rep. Chalmers P. Wylie, of Ohio, had always supported the Reagan administration's position on funding the contras—that is, until the March 1986 vote. *The New York Times* reported that Mr. Wylie "started to sway when the phone calls from his district in Columbus ran significantly against the President."

When calling either the Washington or home office:
● Identify yourself and your affiliation (i.e. a constituent, Oxfam America donor or member of a hunger task force.)
● Ask to speak to the legislative aide handling the issue.
● Keep your message brief. If necessary, send background information on the bill or your position.
Telephone Numbers:
Congressional members: (202)224-3121
The White House: (202) 456-1414
White House Comment Line: (202) 456-7639
Western Union: (800) 325-6000 (20 word opinion telegram is under $5—call for current prices.)

Organizing a Campaign

Before you begin a lobbying campaign in your community, check with other groups working on the same issue. To have an impact on national legislation you need to be working with a national campaign. Several groups provide up-to-date information on legislation facing Congress, advice on effective organizing and resources to help local groups. Bread for the World, the Christian Citizens' lobby, has been organizing people to lobby for hunger-related legislation for more than ten years. Impact, Network, Oxfam America and Results have helpful materials and lobbying networks as well. See the appendix for more information. Most denominations also have a Washington office to co-ordinate lobbying on issues on which they've taken a stand.

Joining in coalition with other local groups that share your concern can greatly increase your impact. But you also need to reach out to people who aren't already members of an organization. Ways to do that include:

Letter-writing campaign. Assemble materials for letter writing— sample letters, important addresses, paper, pens, envelopes and stamps—and pick a busy location such as a shopping mall, the sidewalk in front of the Post Office or school lobby. It's also a good idea to have a flyer explaining your campaign with a name and telephone number for further information.

Literature Tables. Setting up a table in a busy shopping mall or street corner is an effective way to hand out materials, collect signatures for a petition, or obtain names and addresses for future events you may be planning.

Petitions. Petitions are useful when you are trying to build a constituency for a particular issue. With petition in hand, you can talk to people in your community about the issue, the purpose of the petition, the goal of your campaign and how they can get involved. Elected officials pay less attention to petitions than to individual letters, but they can be a valuable way to educate and identify potential supporters. You may be able to arrange media coverage when the petitions are presented, emphasizing the numbers of local signers. (See Chapter 24 on using the media.) Be sure to photocopy the petitions before turning them in so that you can continue to involve the signers in future activities.

Opinion Polls. Use opinion polls to generate newsworthy observations. Consider polling local politicians about their commitment to the homeless and measuring that against their voting record on fair housing issues. Or draw up a simple questionnaire to poll people on the street.

Media. News releases and Letters to the Editor are excellent ways to share your concerns or the results of your opinion poll or petition drive. Respond to specific articles or editorials, especially if you think they present the issue in an unfavorable or uninformed light. See chapter 24 for suggestions on working with the media.

As citizens in a democracy we have both the right and the responsibility to help shape laws that reflect our values and priorities.

For more information on how you can influence public policy through Congress, contact Bread for the World, a Christian citizen's movement that focuses solely on hunger issues: 802 Rhode Island Avenue, N.E., Washington, DC 20018. Or contact Results, a non-religiously based hunger lobby: 245 Second Street, N.E., Washington, DC 20002.

13

Work with State and Local Governments

By Callie Hutchison

Faced with hungry people in our communities many of us have organized to provide emergency food, clothing and shelter. As we become more aware of the root causes of the problems and the need for larger-scale programs, we often turn to *advocacy*, literally calling out to the government for help. That has most often meant lobbying Congress. But Washington can be far away and some of our national leaders seem particularly unreachable.

Too often we bypass our state and local governments, although local and even state leaders tend to be more accessible, and policy changes at the state and local levels are important in feeding hungry people and eliminating causes of hunger in our communities. Successful state and local advocacy can bring significant increases in support for existing programs. In Texas in 1985 advocates helped pass the Omnibus Anti-Hunger Act and gained $11.5 million in state support for WIC, elderly nutrition and emergency services. In Maryland in 1986 advocates pushed for and got nearly $2 million in added support for the school meal program, home delivered meals and the Maryland Food Bank.

Improvements don't always require changes in state or local budgets. In Tennessee advocates passed a law requiring schools with a high percentage of low-income children to participate in the federally-supported School Breakfast Program. The number of schools serving breakfast increased from 20 percent to 75 percent with no additional state or local funding.

Avenues for Change

Ways of changing public policy fit into several categories. The most common is *legislative action*: passing a bill through an elected body. We usually call this lobbying although many aspects of working with elected officials and promoting particular ideas are not technically lobbying. Legislation can change almost any aspect of policy from the amount of money available to who is responsible for administering a program.

Administrative advocacy is an often-neglected route to significant change, particularly for the increase in accessibility of services or increased priority for food and poverty programs. Administrative strategies may preceed or follow legislative action. Changes in budgets, for example, can sometimes be accomplished by citizen input to an agency when it is preparing its budget request. Administrative advocacy in Nashville, Tennessee, opened the way for thousands of homeless people across the state to get food stamps. Federal legislation had already extended food stamp eligibility to people without permanent address, but state and local administrators of the Food Stamp program interpreted the law differently. Local advocates challenged the interpretation and got the procedure clarified.

When all else fails, a lawsuit or the threat of one can move policy makers. *Litigation* can help protect people's rights to services, ensure that regulations are implemented fairly, or challenge rules or procedures. Litigation in Arizona, for instance, forced state officials to obey federal regulations for issuing food stamps quickly to people in emergency situations. Sometimes local authorities see litigation as helpful, since it gives them a reason or the authority to change rules or procedures imposed from above. Programs and services have been saved from budget cuts in some cases because agencies are under court order to maintain a certain level of service.

The *electoral process* is another important way to make changes at the state and local levels. Local elective offices offer more possibilities for participation in and influence of electoral process. Many people ignore state and local races and then wonder why policies are not what they would like to see. Though non-profit organizations are prohibited from endorsing candidates or participating in partisan politics, individuals (except certain government employees) can participate at all levels, and can run for office themselves.

State and Local Advocacy: Get Ready!
Build an information base. Right, fair and reasonable is not enough. Accurate information, a thorough understanding of the issues involved and the ability to communicate what you know are critical.

In some cases research may simply mean gathering information that already exists. If those with the information don't want to share it, insisting on the public's right to know may be an important first step toward making change. In other cases the problem may be lack of information, and you will need to create some of your own data. For instance, attempts to establish the number of homeless people have involved actually going out and counting people. Surveys of program participants have provided information about their unmet needs.

Often policy makers will create a study committee, task force or commission to review the situation, explore alternatives and make recommendations. This kind of approach can establish credibility and public awareness about an issue since a government-appointed body has resources, information and authority beyond those available to your group. Officials can learn about problems, form their own opinions, often sell themselves on the changes that are needed, and become more committed to solving problems. "Studying the issue" can, however, be a way to delay action, derail the issue altogether or re-define the problem with unexpected and sometimes harmful results. The makeup of the committee is critical. The more you can participate in the determination of the committee makeup and influence the process, the more likely you are to be pleased with the outcome.

Use information gathering to clarify specific changes needed. Figure out who will be affected directly (clients and providers) and indirectly (perhaps grocers or farmers), how they will be affected, costs and benefits of the proposed change, supporters and opponents (active, passive and potential), and arguments for and against.

You will also need a thorough understanding of the decision-making process. Research informal processes as well as the on-paper structures so that you will understand how decisions get made long before votes are actually taken. You need to know what body is responsible for the decision, when they will act and how they operate. Who are the key players, and who influences them? Explore options for appealing or changing decisions once they are made.

Develop a workable strategy. Advanced planning is essential. Avoid the temptation to jump into the process as soon as you understand the need. Perhaps you need to meet a critical deadline such as a budget hearing or cut-off time for submitting bills, but when possible slow down. Anticipate future opportunities and allow time for planning and organizing. The key to a good strategy is not how elaborate it is but how specific, concrete and related to the real world you can make it.

Strategic thinking involves setting goals, deciding the best tactics to meet those goals and then drawing up an action plan. Chapter one has suggestions for strategic planning. An excellent book for more detailed ideas is *Lives Matter: a Handbook for Christian Organizing* by Kimberly Bobo. (See appendix.)

Get Set

Involving other people is one key to an effective strategy. Identify individuals and organizations with similar concerns, related interests or expertise or resources helpful to the action plan. Early on you will need to decide who and how many to involve in actual planning and decision making. For a short-term, single-issue goal you may not want to put much effort into structure and organization. If you intend to continue to work on future changes, you need to give serious attention to organizational structure. (See chapter 1.)

For an important reality check involve those who are directly affected by proposed changes when building strategy and making decisions. Will what you are trying to do result in the changes you expect? First-hand experience increases the group's authority when speaking for change. Given an opportunity and encouragement, those with direct experience are often the best spokespeople. Working together across class, race, gender and other dividing lines also breaks down the barriers to change.

A broad base of support increases your group's power, but including more people also takes time and can slow down your action plan. New people bring new ideas that need to be tested against previous plans. They may redefine the issues that require major changes in strategy. Sometimes that is positive and adds elements that were overlooked. Don't change or abandon the group's original goals, however, unless it's clearly a step forward enthusiastically endorsed by the whole group.

Coalition efforts are essential in some cases. When different groups can agree on common goals they often act together. Critically important, each group must understand and communicate its interests and goals. The whole group should agree on leadership, communication and accountability. People and groups can work together without establishing a formal coalition. Spontaneous action from several different sources can be useful at times. Organized and coordinated effort can exert greater leverage. Although it requires much patience, working through issues with another organization contributes to the success of the effort.

Go!

The plan of action may identify a wide variety of possible activities to carry out the strategy. Which to use depends on what is appropriate and practical given the nature of the group and the resources available.

The most common activity is a meeting or series of meetings with state or local officials to identify the problem and develop and negotiate desired changes. Before the meeting plan what you want to accomplish or find out. Decide who will go, and what roles they will play. Try to have as much of the meeting under your group's control as possible, including leadership, location and agenda, but know that you may have to participate in meetings over which you have little control. Being clear about what you want will help you move forward. Be sure to keep records or notes and prepare summaries of all the meetings you attend.

Occasionally, strategies may not be public to keep the potential opposition uninformed and thus unorganized. Most strategies, though, call for building pressure on decision makers by increasing public awareness of the problem and support for your position. Possible ways to increase public pressure include:

Public hearings/candidate forums. Hold your own or attend one called by someone else. The format normally includes written or oral questions and comments. Members of your group can contribute facts and data, personal stories, alternatives to present policies or examples from other states. Many hearings and forums are open to anyone who wishes to speak, but in some cases speakers are determined in advance. Make sure your position is heard at all opportunities and challenge situations when it is not.

Media. Using the media is key to almost any strategy. Feature stories, editorials, letters, commentary and talk shows are good vehicles for your message. See chapter 24 on working with media.

Personal. To influence a particular key decision maker, identify possible pressure points. Find out who knows the person and what kinds of arguments are likely to work. Who are important constituents? Personal pressure happens through phone calls, letters, face to face meetings, and sometimes being a visible presence. Group meetings, telephone trees and letter-writing campaigns multiply the pressure, but remember, they require planning and preparation and should be included in strategy planning.

Special action days. If you have the time and resources, a special day when allies and supporters take a specific action or attend an event can demonstrate unity and a broad base of support. Invite policy makers to attend.

Direct action. Activities such as demonstrations, marches and confrontations often make people uncomfortable, but some situations require dramatic and intense methods to get attention. Lack of power can keep people from being able to participate in policy making processes. Direct action may be necessary to gain enough power to be included in discussions and decisions.

Follow-up

When you reach your goal, you're still not done. A policy or law is only a piece of paper until it's implemented. Monitor to make sure changes are carried out. Evaluate the change to make sure it accomplishes what you intended. If you did not achieve all you set out to do, look at possibilities for future progress. Ask yourself and members of the group what more can be done.

Don't forget to thank supporters and co-workers, including lawmakers who voted in favor of your position. Awards and celebrations are also ways to maintain the support of friendly policy makers and the energy and commitment of those who worked on the campaign.

Feeling overwhelmed?

Remember that advocacy doesn't require experts or professionals although you may wish to consult with people who have specific expertise and encourage them to volunteer their services. Anyone working to change public policy learns by doing it. You may have experience or a key piece of information that will change one vote or even the outcome. Don't assume everyone knows what you know. You have the right and responsibility as a citizen to participate and be heard; elected officials have a responsibility to give your ideas and concerns serious consideration.

Taking action at the state and local level requires a willingness to be seen and heard. We are likely to face disagreements and controversy and may need to learn new skills and undertake new activities. That can take time and be frustrating, but it can also be more enriching and rewarding than you expect. And it may not happen without you.

If you are not ready to organize a fully developed campaign, you can start more modestly.

Look around. What groups in your area work for change in state or local government? Joining one may be a way to gain experience and identify the skills and resources needed. If the group works on related issues you can help them see the need for your specific concern and add it to their agenda.

Set up a task force in an existing organization. If a group you belong to provides direct services to hungry or homeless people, you could initiate work on state and local policy changes through a public policy committee or legislative task force. (See chapter 1.)

Start a discussion group. Get together with friends and interested people to start a group in your church or synagogue or with several congregations. (See chapters 4 and 23.) Include in the study possible ways to take action.

Write, call, talk. Discover the positions of your elected officials. What proposals are they offering? Will they work with you on changes? Express your opinions to them and to co-workers, neighbors, friends and the media.

Don't get discouraged. These struggles are not easy. It's much easier to be cynical or apathetic as many around you no doubt are. Perhaps you've tried and lost. Remember that certain changes have to wait for certain opportunities. Public policy can seem or even *be* whimsical. It's a human process with good days and bad that require equal parts of hard work and dumb luck. Wear them out and wait them out. Persistence and patience may be the key requirements for success.

Hunger is caused by poverty and poverty is related to the lack of power. Whether or not you are successful, your participation changes the process and creates the potential for future success. By participating in state and local government decisions, we help shape the conditions and values under which our community will operate.

In the end it's not something you do to help someone else. The changes you make will help others, but you are working for yourself, too. We work because we want governments that are open and responsible to everyone in the community and because we want to live in communities that are fair and just. We help others to help ourselves.

Food Stamp Outreach

By Jo-Ann Eccher

Food stamps are the nation's primary tool for providing food assistance and the only food program serving entire low-income families. In recent years poverty has increased, yet food stamp coverage has diminished. More than twelve million Americans eligible for food stamps are not participating, which means that 40 percent of the eligible poor are not being served!

With more people hungry and living in poverty, why aren't people applying for food stamp benefits? According to studies by groups as diverse as the President's Task Force on Food Assistance and the Physicians' Task Force on Hunger in America, it's because they lack information about the program and its eligibility requirements. Whole segments of the population—working families, families with children, the elderly, the disabled and the homeless— lack basic information about the food stamp program. Many who were ineligible in the past may now be eligible because of recent changes in the program, but no nationwide federal program or outreach effort lets them know they may be eligible.

Eligibility for most households is determined by gross income below 130 percent of the poverty line and by assets like money in the bank or property owned. In 1986 seventy-eight percent of all food stamp recipients were single heads of housholds, children, elderly or disabled. Of the remaining 22 percent, one-third worked and all others registered for work. The average food stamp benefit is fifty cents per person per meal.

Why Eligible People Don't Participate

In 1977 food stamp program reforms mandated states to use outreach to identify and overcome barriers to participation. In 1981, however, based on the belief that "The American people as a whole are well-informed about the availability of food stamps," that mandate was repealed. Combined with $7 billion in cuts to the program, the elimination of official outreach resulted in an estimated non-participation rate of 40 to 50 percent of those potentially eligible.

At the Project Bread Food Stamp Hotline, an information, referral and advocacy center in Boston, people who call give a variety of reasons for not having applied for food stamps before: I didn't know; I own a house, so I didn't think I could get food stamps; I always thought I had to be on welfare first; My husband works so I didn't think we could get on food stamps; I've always been too scared; I work, so that makes me ineligible, right? The common thread in these replies, the lack of information concerning eligibility, is the greatest barrier to participation.

Recent Efforts to Increase Outreach

Beginning in 1986 the National Advertising Council launched a two-year public service campaign to provide information on the food stamp program. Reaching a national audience through broadcast and print ads and public transit and outdoor posters, the campaign helped increase participation in food stamp and nutrition programs. Because developing outreach materials can be beyond the financial ability of many grassroots food providers, the free brochures, posters and other food stamp campaign materials produced by the Ad Council have increased these groups' ability to do effective outreach. The combined efforts of local groups and the national campaign increased access to the program by informing those who were eligible, removing barriers to participation and increasing communication with food stamp policy makers on the local, state and federal levels.

Outreach is more than getting out material and information. It can't be accomplished by sneaking out in the middle of the night, tacking up a flier and waiting for the phone to ring. The purpose of outreach is to achieve the goals food stamps were set up to accomplish: improve the nutritional status of low income households and thus prevent hunger and malnutrition in this country. To reach these goals, a thorough outreach project will include identifying barriers, monitoring the progress of an applicant through the system and changing policy. A campaign should include direct client advocacy and communications with the Food Stamp Office at the state level and with USDA for policy changes. Ideally, food stamp outreach should be coordinated with outreach campaigns for all food and nutrition programs.

Food stamp outreach therefore means community organizing. The goals are long-range: not simply helping a few more people get foodstamps, but building wide-spread awareness and active concern that can change public policies. Finding, encouraging and supporting poor people to be effective advocates on their own behalf is a key part of the strategy.

Steps to an Effective Outreach Campaign

1. Learn about the food stamp program.

Start with FRAC's updated Guide to the Food Stamp Program (available from FRAC at the address in the appendix). Also available from government bookstores is the Federal Food Stamp Code; CFR 7 parts

210 - 299 ($13.00). An important free resource is your state's food stamp department's budget request to the state legislature. More than numbers, a budget request tells how the program in your state works.

2. Build Coalitions.

Work with poverty rights groups, emergency food providers, food law centers, WIC clinics, churches and other groups concerned with food. Inform local welfare offices of your efforts. Don't forget to include food stamp front-line workers in your communications. If you work just at the director level, local workers may not learn of your efforts until clients begin appearing at their offices complete with your outreach material.

3. Develop your own targeted materials when necessary.

You may need material dealing with clients rights and responsibilities, food stamps and homelessness, or expedited issuance (emergency food stamps). You may wish to develop your own forms for prescreening and monitoring, a verification checklist, and training materials.

4. Assess your community.

How your campaign proceeds will depend on which groups you target. Identify those in your community not participating in the food stamp program using community statistics such as poverty figures, unemployment, federal food program participation rates and emergency food use. Targets can include low-income working families, unemployed families, public assistance families, the homeless, emergency food recipients, the elderly, the rural poor and non-English speaking households. (See chapter 6 for suggestions on community surveys.)

5. Use the outreach methods that are effective for your target group.

Outreach methods are quite varied, as indicated below, and can be mixed and matched. Stick to those that are reasonable, affordable and achievable for your group. Some methods your group might want to try include:

Training on the food stamp program for community groups such as emergency food providers and health workers so they can inform their clients about food stamp eligibility and benefits. Training should include basic information about food stamps and who is eligible; factors that affect eligibility, including household size and presence of students, elderly or disabled people; income and resource limits; how to apply for the program and verify eligibility; special cases, like the homeless, strikers or people without identification; and how to make referrals to local food stamp offices.

Prescreening sessions for potential applicants. Prescreen for eligibility at emergency food sites, federal commodity distribution sites, WIC clinics or churches. Before doing the prescreening contact the agency and distribute flyers announcing the day your group will be prescreening. Arrange space for one person to answer general food stamp questions and distribute materials and another space where prescreenings can occur in private.

At the prescreening itself answer questions about the food stamp program; distribute materials on food stamps and application procedures; assess the applicant's eligibility; assist applicants in locating verification; and refer those who are eligible to the appropriate local food stamp office.

After the prescreening encourage applicants to report successes and barriers in applying and receiving food stamps to your group or agency sponsoring the prescreening session. Systematically document barriers and report to local, state and federal officials to bring about policy changes.

Media work can be an effective form of outreach. Work with local broadcast and print media, including the neighborhood weeklies. Don't overlook cable stations. (See chapter 24.) Have your mayor or legislator endorse the outreach campaign at a press conference. Don't overlook newsletters and community bulletins as a way to spread the word.

Set up a telephone information and referral system for people to ask questions about food stamps. People can ask questions about the program, get information about applying and receive advocacy help when benefits are denied. Simply telling people about food stamps is not necessarily going to help them overcome the barriers encountered at the food stamp office.

Mini-grants are available from some states and private foundations to community groups to increase food stamp participation. Legislation in Massachusetts, for instance, makes grants ranging from $3,000 to $7,000 available to local community groups for production and distribution of literature and other forms of outreach. Grants also give community groups formal status, allowing them access to the Department of Public Welfare. This enhances their role as a place outside the bureaucracy where clients can ask questions about food stamps and find people who can guide them through the bureaucracy.

Distribute materials at targeted sites such as grocery stores, emergency food centers, housing projects, health centers, WIC clinics or commodity distribution sites.

Use door-to-door canvassing to reach the elderly at home or hard-to-reach people.

Hold public forums on food stamps to educate the public and counteract the myths that cause stigma.

Act as an ombudsman and advocate to document barriers and bring about food stamp policy changes. Oppose further cuts or changes in regulations that would adversely affect participation. Call for reinstatement of federal funds for information and outreach.

Monitoring and evaluation will help you identify successes and mistakes. Do not overlook this step. Continuous information gathering is a powerful tool in advocacy efforts and in finding new ways to reach low-income people. Ask groups you train to report to you how many people they are referring to the food stamp office. Ask a local food stamp office to find where applicants heard about food stamps. Ask the local food stamp office director if there has been an increase in applications. Set up a phone bank to call people you prescreen for food stamps. Did they apply? Were they eligible? Did they receive food stamps? Document barriers and communicate them to policy makers. Barriers can include:

• Physical access to the program. Access can be increased or denied by office hours, staffing, availability of staff for home visits or phone interviews for elderly and disabled and access to public transportation.

• The application process. Everyone has the right to apply: Are people being verbally denied this right? Also find out if people are informed of same-day filing and whether emergency (expedited) food stamps are given to families in dire need.

• The verification process. Find out if offices are requiring excessive verification or failing to assist clients in locating sources of verification. Offices should accept collateral contacts, that is, a statement from someone who knows the client's circumstances.

• Fair hearing practices. People who are denied food stamp benefits are supposed to be informed of their right to examine their files and to have a fair hearing with people from the food stamp office who have not been involved with the action taken against them.

The Project Bread Food Stamp Hotline in Boston presents this documentation to the Massachusetts Department of Public Welfare, the Governor's Planning Committee on Homelessness, Massachusetts Law Reform and the state's congressional delegation. Their efforts have brought about a coordinated, progressive policy stance in improving Massachusetts residents' access to food stamps. Documentation helped them develop material targeted to the homeless and in a number of languages, led to training for workers at local offices in the treatment of clients and resulted in clearer policies for the homeless. The documentation of outreach efforts has also helped Project Bread in testifying to the House Committee on Agriculture and the House Select Committee on Hunger.

Target Your Outreach
The following groups in your community may be in need of outreach. Here are the methods that are likely to be most effective in reaching them.

Low-income families with children.
Working families make up the greatest increase in numbers of poor over the last four years with an increase of 66 percent. Children under six years are particularly vulnerable to the long-term effects of undernutrition. The food stamp program is the only program targeted to improve nutrition for the whole family.

Outreach: Distribute materials at WIC clinics, school lunch, school breakfast, community health centers, Head Start programs, churches and grocery stores. Information and Referral phonelines, advocacy efforts and targeted mailings are also helpful.

Unemployed families

Many unemployed families are new to the public assistance system and do not know points of entry, and half the people suffering from unemployment are children.

Outreach: The methods given above for families are appropriate. Also pass out information at unemployment lines, unemployed unions, grocery stores, job fairs and emergency food sites.

The elderly

Elders, particularly elderly women, make up 50% of those eligible but not participating.

Outreach: Provide training for home health agencies. Target educational campaigns at senior meal sites. Develop materials with easy-to-read print. Provide transportation to food stamp offices for elders. Inform elders of their right to waive a face-to-face interview and to be interviewed for food stamps in their home.

The homeless

Homeless people are nutritionally at risk because of exposure to environment and dependency on soup kitchens for meals. They need special advocacy campaigns to assure their access to the program despite lack of a permanent address.

Outreach: Distribute information at homeless shelters and soup kitchens, bus stations and travelers aide offices. Serve an advocacy/ombudsman role for gaining state policy clarification that homeless persons have the right to food stamps and to document cases where homeless people are denied food stamps because they reside in a shelter that is serving two or more meals. USDA defines shelters as institutions and therefore denies food stamps to individuals living in shelters. Lobby Congress to change the institutional status of shelters for the homeless. Prescreen for food stamp eligibility at shelters and meal programs. Train shelter providers and soup kitchen workers on food stamp eligibility and benefit programs. Work for acceptance of the use of stamps by homeless people in restaurants.

Emergency and commodity food recipients.

Emergency food recipients are diverse: families and individuals, black, white, hispanic and oriental, young and old. Emergency food recipients lack money to buy food, and their numbers are growing.

Outreach: Distribute information at food banks, food pantries and commodity distribution points. Train emergency providers on food stamp benefits, eligibility and referral. Prescreen on site and make referrals. Equip information and referral phonelines with advocates to walk clients through the system over the phone.

Recipients of public assistance, AFDC and SSI.

In many states up to 30 per cent of AFDC households and 70 per cent

of SSI households don't receive food stamps although the law gives them categorical food stamp eligibility.
Outreach: Target mailings to all AFDC and SSI households. Use the "tell a friend about food stamps" approach. Distribute materials through welfare rights groups.

Non-English speaking households.
Language barriers prevent participation.
Outreach: Provide translation services; translate materials. Work for changes in regulations so that materials will be available in a number of appropriate languages.

Fuel assistance recipients.
Poor people frequently face the choice of "Heat or eat."
Outreach: Distribute materials at fuel assistance agencies. Work for regulations allowing local utilities to include food stamp information in their billings.

Newly divorced women.
One out of every four married middle-class women will divorce and fall into poverty.
Outreach: Distribute food stamp program information at legal services and women's centers.

Part Four

Live Responsibly

I sit on man's back, choking him and making him carry me and yet assure myself and others that I am sorry for him and wish to lighten his load by all possible means except by getting off his back.

—Leo Tolstoy

Responsible living, simple living, living with less. Whatever we call it, we must take responsibility for our own use of resources. Responsible living isn't a list of *do's* and *don'ts*, but what we are living *for*—a less selfish, more faithful way to journey through this world.

For many of us, accumulating staggering mountains of gadgets, habits and debts is as easy as saying "Charge it." Thousands of well-paid people sit around thinking up new gadgets and habits to sell us, and we accept their ideas on how to use our money and time. Long after the advertisers, retailers, recruiters and polluters have extracted their pound of flesh, we still don't know what we've given away.

Where do we invest the brief 24 hours, seven days, 52 weeks, 70 or so years of our lives? Where do we channel our limited money? How much do we choose to spend, give away, save? To whom will we listen, what books will we read? What issues will we allow to touch and move us? What resources do we need, and what unneeded ones do we consume? Can we learn to distinguish wants from needs?

We are bound in a complicated web to fellow human beings and other creatures on this tiny planet. How can we live responsibly in a world where many people don't have even basic necessities? No one decisive act can free us from manipulated, cluttered lives, enabling instant responsibility. The sum of a lifetime of small decisions will measure who we are.

Chapters in this section will lead you toward more responsible personal living and help you move the organizations around you toward more faithful collective responsibility.

15

Live for People Not Things

By Gary Gunderson and Tom Peterson

What used to be called "simple living" offered the vision of sharing resources with needy people while freeing ourselves from the burdens of conformity and over-consumption. But few of us are ready to renounce our lifelong search for security and enthusiastically embrace freedom and responsibility. Obligations hold us back, and "simple living" can be terribly complicated and time-consuming. Our minor, symbolic changes seem insignificant in the face of the world's overwhelming needs. We muddle toward integrity, feeling guilty, naive and a bit silly.

Yet muddling may be a sensible way to act. Problems of hunger and poverty, energy and environment often feel confusing and overwhelming because they *are*, in fact, confusing and overwhelming. We absorb vast amounts of emotionally devastating information and try to make difficult decisions balancing conflicting values. Facing an array of urgent issues, we are often tempted to flee.

Muddling, as a means of struggle, does not inspire the warm glow of pride we'd like, but at least we muddlers are in good and abundant company. We can't abstain from muddling because life is too complicated, but we *can* choose to muddle in the right directions.

Values and Standards

To break through old habits and assumptions we have to *intentionally upset the balance of tensions* in our lives. Begin by looking inward. The following questions may offer some insights.

● How does my standard of living compare to my parents'? Consider money, food and shelter, education, financial security, health.

● Do my possessions make me happy? Why or why not?

● Do I use possessions I still expect to have five years from now? How many possessions do I *never* use?

● How many things within 50 feet of me are made from materials that cannot or will not be used again?

● If a third world person visited me, would she or he think my lifestyle is responsible?

- Do I expect my children to be affected by shortages of basic materials like oil? How do I contribute to, or refuse to cooperate in creating those shortages?
- Looking at the whole world and at future generations, can I say I'm using my fair share?

Starters

"Okay," you say. "Maybe I've got a problem. I'd like to look my grandchildren in the eye and not feel that I've stolen their future. What do I do about all the clutter in my life? Where do I start?"

- Substitute permanent items for throw-aways, such as cloth napkins for paper or recycle your newspapers. Use permanent rather than styrofoam cups.
- Commit to missing one meal a week for a month. Use the time for reflection and give the money to hunger causes.
- Go through your clothes closet. Give away anything you haven't worn for at least 2 years. Do the same in the kitchen and hobby area. If you don't use it, give it to someone who will. Don't try to make money—you benefit by cutting the clutter. If you have to sell something, give the money away.
- Eliminate 10 miles of car travel this week by cutting out or combining trips. If each mile costs 25 cents, you'll save $10 in one month. Send the money to a local ecology group.
- Do something for somebody today that costs less than 25 cents and takes less than half an hour. Help weave the net of neighborly love: Send a brief note, take a child for a walk, pick a flower, mow an elderly friend's lawn (free—maybe 50 cents in gas), visit a neighbor.
- Unplug the TV and put an attractive tablecloth over it, forcing yourself to at least hesitate before letting the monster drone your life away. Count the programs you do watch, particularly noting the commercials and their impact on your spending habits.
- Read a good lifestyle book. You might start with Richard Foster's *Freedom of Simplicity.*

Shopping

If Mother Earth could speak, she'd probably thank us if we all took a break from buying things for a couple of decades to give her a chance to recover from our commercial onslaught. But our lives go on, and we continue to need things. Which are essential? How do we balance "simplicity" and convenience? Before you buy, consider:

- Will this purchase affect my grandchildren's opportunity to have the same resources I inherited?
- Does this product damage the environment? Did its manufacture? Will its disposal?
- Is rental or co-ownership an option? Do I need it all to myself?
- Is another model more efficient or durable? Responsible living can

mean fewer purchases of higher quality goods.
- Can the item I'm replacing be repaired?
- Will this purchase help me be more responsible (or less) in coming years? What patterns am I establishing? Will they make me more or less joyful, thankful, sensitive to my inter-relatedness with the earth and other people?

Food

Most of us in the United States eat more than we need, and we suffer health problems as a result. Adult Americans are 2.3 billion pounds overweight — that's 20.9 pounds per person. We eat too much, and we eat the wrong things. Many foods on supermarket shelves are not healthy, and foods imported to the United States can cause suffering of third world people. Coffee, for example, is often grown on land that could grow food. Some guidelines:
- Eat fewer processed, "convenience" foods. Most food price increases in recent years are from processing that also often adds harmful additives. About a billion pounds of additives are processed into our food each year—4.5 pounds per person. Snack foods are a major villain. Try fruit, nuts or carrots instead.
- Have simpler meals. Rediscover soup with bread and fruit.
- Eat less meat. The average American eats twice as much protein as the body needs. While nutritionists recommend that ⅔ of our protein come from vegetables and grains, most of us get ¾ from meat. Beans or dairy products combined with grains provide complete protein, often with less cholesterol and fat than meat. The meat on our tables also represents about 2,000 pounds of grain a year for each of us, fed to the animals that feed us. The average African or Asian has access to 400 pounds of grain a year and eats corn or rice instead of meat.
- Reduce consumption of coffee, sugar and alcohol: They don't do you any good, and the land that produced them could grow real food.
- Grow your own. Plant fruit trees as well as tomatoes, and help feed the next generation.
- Avoid waste through careful planning and smaller portions. One fourth of the food we bring home is never eaten; 49 billion people could live on what Americans throw away.

Clothes

"Clothes make the man," they told us, and we bought it. Even those of us who don't aspire to be men. A few ways to reduce our urgent concerns:
- Keep a smaller, more basic, less faddish wardrobe.
- Sew and mend. Wear clothes until they wear out.
- When you buy, buy quality. Clothes that fall apart after a few washings are no bargain.
- Recycle. There's nothing wrong with second-hand clothes, and shopping thrift stores can be a great adventure. Trade with neighbors and

friends. Have a giant "clothes swap" at your church or club.
- Take advantage of off-season specials.
- Avoid designer gizmos that add price rather than quality.

WARNING: Do not expect your children's enthusiastic cooperation. Kids are feeling enormous pressure to conform in clothing at ever-younger ages. Is your simplicity bought at the cost of your child's tears and feelings of isolation? Can you arrive at compromises that you both feel okay about?
- Don't wear fur. It may be a status symbol, but the original owners have more right to their hides than you do.

Cars

The average American rides or drives more than 8,000 miles a year. In a world of limited resources and growing pollution, we consume far more than our fair share of energy, much of it in transportation. Some alternatives:
- Relearn the art of walking.
- Ride a bicycle. Three out of five car trips in this country are less than five miles. A bicycle is the most efficient transportation for short distances, provides healthy exercise and doesn't pollute.
- Use mass transit: Next to bicycling it's the most energy-efficient way to travel.
- Carpool. Save money and energy and make friends while learning the art of conflict resolution.

Money

Use of money is the bottom line in nearly all ethical matters. Advertisers understand better than we that no matter what we say we believe, proof comes when we put down our money. How do we bring our money use under responsible control?
- Kick money off the throne of your life. Money is a tool that can enable or obstruct responsibility. Nothing more. Nothing less. Money itself has no value, but as we use it, we express *our* values. Before spending, ask yourself what this use of money says about your values. That doesn't mean be a miser. A friend's guideline for simple living was never to own more than 500 things. (A spoon or a sock counted as one "thing.") Despite his radical simplicity, he found that thinking about "things" dominated his life. That's not the point.
- When possible, avoid debt. Hesitate long before spending future options on present gratification.
- Teach your children responsible money habits. Gradually raise your child's allowance to cover luxuries and necessities so that by the age of sixteen she/he will have learned to manage all income and expenses except housing and food.
- Consider a voluntary "fair share tax." We know one serious jogger who, whenever he spends money on shoes or equipment, writes a check for the same amount to world hunger. "My ability to run reflects my

enormous privileges of a safe neighborhood, access to good health care, a job with decent hours and enough money to eat well. The least I can do is tax myself so I carry more of my fair share."

Mazon, a Jewish hunger organization, encourages Jews to contribute 3 percent of what they spend on special celebrations like *bar mitzvah*. Some people tax themselves for all imported or luxury foods they buy and give that money to support development or human rights efforts in third world countries.

● How much do you give away? The Biblical starting point is the tithe—one tenth of our income. But that may be far too low: 10 percent of a $10,000 income is a substantial contribution, 10 percent of a million dollar income barely cuts into discretionary income. Some families set a basic level of income they need to live reasonably then give away a higher percentage of each thousand dollars earned above that. If you do not want an increase in income to automatically change your standard of living, consider giving away the bulk of new funds that come to you.

● What is your investment money doing? Does your bank loan money in your community? What about stocks and bonds? (See chapter 16 for more on responsible investments.)

Television

Saint Paul warns, "Do not be conformed to this world, but be transformed by the renewing of your mind." But Paul never had to cope with television. Being conformed is exactly what TV is all about. Most of us enjoy TV, but we need to be aware of its grip. The average American watches well over 27 hours of TV a week, and children see even more. (You don't think this applies to you? Keep a log for a couple of weeks and be amazed.) Average toddlers will spend more time in front of a television before they start school than they will spend in classrooms for the rest of their lives. People are rightly concerned about violence on TV, but what about other values television teaches?

Richard Foster says in *Freedom of Simplicity* "Taken as a whole, media commercials constitute a world view, a real religious philosophy about what constitutes blessedness. Television tells us that the most idiotic things will make us insanely happy. They may well make us insane, but I doubt they will ever make us happy." The TV set is the American "family altar." We gather before it nightly while it entertains, informs, and subtly molds us. Says Foster, "We are taken in, duped, brainwashed—but in such subtle ways that we do not realize what has happened. We think we are wise because we see through the childish logic of the commercials. But the ad writer never intended us to believe those silly commercials, only to desire the product they advertise. And sure enough we buy, because the commercials accomplish their goal of inflaming our desire."

Clearly television opens incredible channels of information and communication. With TV, we can instantly know what's happening to people all over the globe. What do we do? Throw it out? Blow it up? A few suggestions:

- Limit family viewing hours. Watch only the best (educational?) programs, and discuss the meanings, values, and viewpoints expressed.
- Notice advertising. Discuss the effect with family members. Do you want things now that you never knew existed before and never missed?
- Find better ways to entertain yourself. Take a walk, read, invite friends over, talk to each other, play with the children, raise hamsters, plant a garden. Painting, weaving, playing musical instruments, baking bread are all activities that don't pollute the mind, nor does volunteer work with a service organization.
- Get a copy of Frances Moore Lappé's *What to Do After You Turn Off the TV.* (See appendix.)

These are but a few of the hundreds of ways we can choose to live freer, more responsible lives. For instance, homeowners directly control more than a fifth of all energy use in the United States. From weatherstripping to wood stoves, we need to consider our living space. What about solar energy? Why not hardwood floors with wool throw rugs? (Synthetic carpets, made from oil, don't decompose when thrown away.)

Disentangling ourselves from the clutter of our lives is no magical process. It happens slowly, through learning, when we confront and change the long-standing destructive patterns in our lives. Gaining control may not feel natural at first, but we must teach ourselves and our children new patterns and habits to organize ourselves for freedom and interdependence. No matter how clever we are about reclaiming our lives, we will always have more to do. But we *can* reduce the clutter that threatens to smother us. When we free ourselves, we leave our children a better, richer, more fulfilling world.

For more ideas, resources and help in responsible living and celebrations, contact Alternatives, Box 429, Ellenwood, GA 30049. (404) 961-0102.

16

Invest Money Responsibly

By Louis L. Knowles

Money is an important tool in the fight against hunger. In the form of donations it buys food and supports programs. But the money we invest, as well as that we give away, can help people break out of poverty. Or it can support institutions and policies that keep people poor and hungry.

Fighting hunger involves changing the policies that create and perpetuate poverty. Chapters 12 and 13 deal with ways to influence Federal, state and local government policies. Banks and conglomerates, however, make vital decisions every day about world trade, crop patterns, fertilizer production and a host of other food-related subjects. How can we impact decisions made in the boardrooms of private corporations where we have no direct voice or vote?

One way is the boycott. Many people participated in the Nestle boycott that forced changes in that international corporation's marketing of infant formula. When a company resists change on a significant moral issue, a boycott can be a justifiable and effective tactic. But boycotts work only when used sparingly, and some corporations are not vulnerable to consumer boycotts.

A less spectacular but equally important strategy is ethical investing: acting on the ethical implications of investment decisions.

Through checking and savings accounts, money market funds and mutual funds, individuals and organizations allow corporations to use their money. The money may be helping to build MX missiles or exploiting people in developing countries. Investors generally worry only about the security and financial returns of investments, not what a corporation is producing or the results of its practices.

The ethical investment movement challenges bankers and money managers who don't believe ethical judgments should be part of investment decisions. To exclude such considerations is in itself an ethical judgment that the financial system works for the common good and that the individual investor need not be concerned with the specifics of how the money is invested.

A Short History of Socially Responsible Investing

Like many other important social and political ideas, ethical investing grew out of the ferment of the 1960s. People noticed that the capital market (the financial system which moves money around) suffered from the same institutional racism afflicting other social systems. Black people and poor people were systematically denied their fair share of capital for reasons that often seemed morally neutral. For example, certain neighborhoods seemed to be bad risks for home mortgages, so the savings banks drew big red lines around them on their maps and stopped making mortgages in those areas. They considered "red-lining" to be prudent and businesslike, even though racial minority communities were disproportionately affected. The civil rights movement and later the ethical investment movement pointed out that the end result of all these "morally neutral" decisions was racial discrimination far more insidious than anything practiced by the Ku Klux Klan.

People also noticed that some corporations profited from arms sales, operations in Apartheid South Africa or policies that reduced the cost of doing business by throwing wastes into rivers and leaky landfills. Church people, labor union leaders and community organizers worked to bring ethical concerns to bear on investment policies. Recognizing the value of entrepreneurship and a free market operating within ethical boundaries, the movement has focused on those corporate leaders whose pursuit of money and power has blinded them to important ethical issues.

Meanwhile, people concerned about hunger and poverty were trying to find ways to channel more investment funds to low-income people who wanted to start their own businesses. Black activist James Forman dramatized this issue in 1969 when he presented the Black Manifesto to U.S. churches, demanding $500 million in investment funds for the creation of black-controlled enterprises including publishing houses, television stations, a land bank and a university. The churches never gave anywhere near $500 million to minority enterprise, but the seed of an idea was planted. Today people continue seeking ways to use investment funds to further businesses operated by low-income people and other disadvantaged groups.

Ethical investors today both *divest*—pull money out of corporations engaged in unjust practices—and *invest* in ways which help low-income people.

Almost Everybody Invests

You don't have to be a big investor before acting to ensure that your money supports the same things you do. Start with your checking and savings accounts. If your accounts are in a regular commercial bank, ask your banker about their investment policies. If you are not satisfied with the answer, consider moving your accounts to a credit union in your neighborhood or place of work. Credit unions are legally restricted as to where they can loan (invest) their despositors' money, and you can easily find out how your money is used. For example, the Self-Help Credit Union in Durham, North Carolina, makes loans across the state to democratically managed workplaces, including cooperatives and worker-owned businesses. If you are particularly interested in cooperatives, further information is available from Co-op America, a membership organization for cooperatives. Contact them at 2100 M Street, N.W., Suite 605, Washington, DC 20063. Or telephone them at (202) 872-5307.

A small industry of financial experts now exists to provide ethical investment services to institutions and individuals. Imagine a church that currently keeps its savings in a money market account which invests heavily in U. S. Treasury securities. The bank is using the church's money to finance the national debt, most of which can be attributed in one way or another to preparations for warfare. If the church moved its funds to a socially responsible bank such as South Shore Bank in Chicago or the American Indian National Bank, the congregation could be financing local business in a racially-mixed community or on an Indian reservation. And the return on its money would be about the same.

Socially Responsible Money Market and Mutual Funds

It's hard for the average individual to shop around nationally for banks that are socially responsible, so many turn to the new socially responsible money market and mutual funds, which combine professional management with social criteria for choosing specific investments. These funds have done quite well financially, showing that good ethics can also be good business.

Below are several options for large and small investors. Readers can write to each of them for a complete prospectus which will explain in detail how the funds work.

Calvert Social Investment Fund
1700 Pennsylvania Avenue NW
Washington, DC 10006
800-368-2745
(In Washington, DC area, dial 951-4800.)

A large financial organization, Calvert offers several ways for an individual or institution to invest. The Social Investment Fund, created in 1982, offers both a money market fund and a stock and bond mutual fund. Calvert searches out companies that are sensitive to environmental concerns, deal fairly with their workers, support equal opportunity and affirmative action for women and minorities, and value creativity. Calvert also avoids investments in nuclear power and corporations involved in South Africa or whose main products are weapons.

Pax World Fund
224 State Street

Portsmouth, NH 03801
(603) 431-8022

For people deeply concerned about peace who believe the U.S. military establishment is out of control, the Pax fund is an attractive option. Pax invests in corporations that do no defense contracting. With assets of more than $74 million, Pax is a stock and bond fund, which means the investor should be prepared to ride out the ups and downs of the markets. However, Pax has done well, generally staying at or above the performance of the stock market. Over the past five years Pax has averaged a 16.12 percent annual rate of return. A Pax World Fund account can be opened with $250, and you can withdraw your money when you need it by sending a letter with a signature verified by a local bank. The fund has seven days from the time it receives your letter to get the money to you.

Working Assets
230 California Street
San Francisco, CA 94111
(800) 533-FUND

This money market fund was established in 1983 by young financial professionals concerned about the ethics of investing. It invests only in short-term, interest-bearing securities which are among the safest types of investments. The fund avoids corporations that are primarily defense contractors, that deal in South Africa or other countries with oppressive governments, are heavy polluters, involved in nuclear power, or anti-labor. They seek out banks doing a good job with economic development in low-income communities.

Since September of 1983 Working Assets has soared from zero to over $100 million in assets. A minimum deposit of $1,000 is required to open an account, and interest rates are competitive with other money market funds. You can withdraw your money at any time with a check or a phone call.

The Dreyfus Third Century Fund, Inc.
600 Madison Avenue
New York, NY 10022
(800) 645-6561

Created in 1972, Dreyfus is the largest of the social investment funds. Concerned about the environment, occupational health and safety, consumer protection and equal opportunity, the fund has the least stringent criteria of those listed. Investments in defense contractors have made it the target of criticism from some investment activists. Minimum investment is $2,500.

South Shore Bank Money Market Accounts
7054 South Jeffrey Boulevard
Chicago, Illinois 60649
(312) 288-1000

South Shore has been unusual among commercial banks for many years in its strong support for economic development in Chicago's inner city. Money market accounts have helped finance redevelopment of low-income minority neighborhoods in the South Shore area of Chicago. Accounts are available with a minimum deposit of $2,500.

Ecumenical Development Cooperative Society
475 Riverside Dr., 10th floor
New York, NY 10115

For those wishing to loan money directly to enterprises operated by low-income people in developing countries, a fourth possibility is the Ecumenical Development Cooperative Society (EDCS). This group was set up by the international ecumenical community in the mid-1970's to channel investment funds from the developed world into developing countries. Currently $13 million is invested in projects such as aquaculture in China, cooperatives in Chile, pig production in Columbia and a fish processing plant in Maine.

Because EDCS provides loans for periods of several years at low interest rates, investors should not expect to get rich. The last time EDCS paid a dividend was in 1984, and then it was only two percent. The investor accepts a modest return and a lack of liquidity in order to have the funds go to work in the poorest corners of the world.

For More Information

In recent years several new firms offering socially reponsible fund managment and/or investment advice have emerged. A directory of firms and individual brokers is available for $8 from the Social Investment Forum. The Interfaith Center for Corporate Responsibility publishes a Directory of Alternative Investments. Cost is $10 for church groups which are members of the Center, $25 for those that are not, and $100 for foundations and corporations. A third directory is available from the Funding Exchange for $5. (See appendix for addresses.)

These funds are but tiny drops of water in the vast financial investment ocean. Socially responsible investors are far from being able to claim credit for major changes in corporate policy, but organizations which combine financial professionalism with good ethics are a hopeful sign. Like the tiny cloud which Elijah saw on the horizon after a long drought, the social investment industry can grow into a force to rain down justice on the world.

17

Help Institutions Be Responsible Too

*By Gary Gunderson, Tom Peterson,
Gruce Winn and Leslie Withers*

Any organization that raises and spends money, owns or rents a building, or serves meals can decide to use the resources it controls in responsible ways. The results will be more to share with those in need or to preserve for future generations, as well as a growing sense of inter-connectedness and responsibility. You can provide encouragement and advice wherever you have a voice: in your workplace, your church or synagogue, your school, your club or civic group.

Though religious groups in particular have strong mandates to use resources wisely and share them freely, they can, in fact, be as selfish and short-sighted as any other group of humans. All too many churches, for instance, spend more on the *interest* on the mortgages on their fine new buildings than they spend on all mission work and benevolence combined. Then those same buildings stand idle most of the week while daycare centers struggle with high commercial rents and the local Girls Club looks in vain for an indoor site for its summer program.

Here are some starting points for institutional responsibility.

Building and Grounds

● Conduct an energy audit. Does the building need storm windows? More insulation? Are the heating and cooling systems energy-efficient? Consider leaving some rooms unheated when not in use. Point out that spending money to make the building energy-efficient can both save money in the long run and help preserve scarce energy resources.

● Grounds can be both attractive and reflect environmental concerns. Consider planting a garden or fruit trees and donating produce to the local food bank. (See chapter 20.)

● Consider making the building available to other organizations that need the space. Also check whether it is accessible to people with physical handicaps. Laws now require accessibility in many kinds of buildings. Remember the building will never be fully useful when some people can't even get inside.

● If your congregation is considering a building program or major capital improvements, ask first whether it's really essential or whether the money might be spent more responsibly in helping other people. If it is essential, consider tithing or matching the money raised and using those funds in projects that help poor and hungry people.

Food

Serving food may not be the most important function of a church or business, but meals are significant. From daily snacks for preschoolers to Wednesday night church suppers to annual awards dinners, food is woven into our lives together. In a world where so many are hungry and malnourished, none of us should be complacent about how much we eat, how much we waste, and the relationships between our greed and our neighbor's need. And when so many suffer serious health problems from eating too much and the wrong foods, we need to help each other establish healthier patterns. Religious groups and those concerned with hunger and nutrition have a particular responsibility to model good stewardship of our bodies and of food resources. The good news is that changes can be interesting, variety in menus and recipes can be pleasing, and sharing our food with sisters and brothers in need helps us feel better about ourselves as well.
Some suggestions:
● Changes in food service require careful planning, patience and per-severance. Make gradual changes in the kinds and amounts of food served.
● Use guidelines established by nutritionists and the U.S. Department of Agriculture in selecting kinds of food to be served. Your local Dietetic Association or County Extension Service may give professional advice in planning meals that are healthy and reflect wise stewardship of food resources. Generally, the guidelines recommend limiting calorie intake to maintain ideal weight; eating a variety of foods, including more fruits, vegetables and whole grains; eating less sugar and salt and highly processed foods; and limiting saturated fat (butter, red meat, hard cheese) and cholesterol (animal products, egg yolks, ice cream). (See chapter 15 for more information about how the food we eat affects us and people in the Third World.)
● Have fun with different kinds of menus. Plan a salad bar, with soup, bread or baked potato for a simple, healthy meal. Or have a "create your own soup" meal. Set out several pots of steaming, seasoned broth: chicken, beef, tomato, or others. Then set out cooked grains and pasta, bite-sized pieces of meat, beans, chopped vegetables and garnishes. Add several kinds of bread, preferably homemade, for another low-cost, healthy meal.
● Kool-Aid and cookies have had their day! If you serve snacks to children, consider this thought from the *More-With-Less Cookbook* by Doris Longacre: "Handing out sugar-filled snack foods and drinks is like giving a stone when your child asks for bread. Sadly, once a child gets used to sugary snacks he may no longer ask for bread." A sugary snack may satisfy the hunger of the moment but supplies no real

nourishment: a "toy food" in contrast to real food like bread, fruit and vegetables. Growing evidence also suggests that some learning disorders and emotional problems in children may be caused or worsened by high-sugar diets. Alternatives include celery and carrot sticks, apple wedges and cubes of cheese, whole grain crackers, bread sticks and pretzels, orange sections, dried fruit, or banana bread.

• Coffee and sweet rolls aren't any better. Like routine snacks for children, most adult snack foods fail to supply real nourishment. The snack foods suggested above for children are equally good for adults, along with assortments of raw vegetables and dip, mixtures of peanuts and raisins, herb teas, hot or cold cider, tomato or V-8 juice. Introduce new foods by offering them as choices along with familiar ones. For a start, offer one non-sweet and one non-caffeine beverage whenever refreshments are served.

These suggestions about cooking for groups are from Grace Winn's book, *Simply Delicious,* which also has a large selection of recipes useful in churches and other institutions. See the appendix for details.

Work and Money

Working for change within institutions is an opportunity to make powerful connections between seemingly neutral business decisions such as choosing a bank, hiring a janitor or doing business with a particular supplier and the impact of those decisions on poor and hungry people in this country and overseas.

• Examine hiring practices within the organization. Insist that those responsible for hiring make a deliberate effort to hire, train and provide support for people who would otherwise not have a job. Those who have been in prison or "on welfare," have physical handicaps or who are the "wrong" race, sex, or age often are not given a fair chance. Or, if hired, they are not given the support and training that will enable them to succeed or advance.

• What about salary levels? This is a touchy but important concern to raise. Some people may be working for such low pay that the organization, in fact, adds its employees to the ranks of hungry people. One large service organization with an international reputation for its work on human rights and economic justice was horrified to discover that many workers in the mail house that sent out their fund appeals were on food stamps because their wages left them below the poverty line.

Also examine the highest salaries paid. We live in a culture where it's not easy to say that a high salary is unjust, and we lack clear standards for what is too high, even among nonprofits. Start by looking to see if salaries are in line with what similar organizations are paying. The ratio between the highest and lowest salary paid is another way to consider whether salaries are fair. If you are on a decision-making level within the organization, insist that questions like this at least be considered.

● Look at finances. Is the organization's money deposited in banks that practice redlining or invested in stocks of companies dumping hazardous waste in someone's back yard? Examine not only cash reserves but also pension funds, endowments, etc. (See chapter 16 for suggestions on responsible investment.) For information on the policies of specific banks and corporations your firm does business with, write the Interfaith Center for Corporate Responsibility at the address in the appendix.

In 1985 Oxfam America withdrew its money from a Boston bank because of its loans to the South African government. Although the bank has since changed its lending policy, Oxfam opted to continue depositing its $3 million with U.S. minority-owned banks pursuing socially responsible investments and making hard-to-get loans to minority businesses and home buyers. Multiply the impact of responsible investment decisions by publicizing them through local media. (See chapter 24 on using the media.).

● Institutional support is essential for many hunger-related projects from a food bank to a local hunger walk. If you work in the corporate world, look at your firm's policies for support of worthy causes. You may be able to nominate projects you work with to receive corporate donations. Some companies match donations made by their employees to nonprofit organizations. Larger firms will sometimes also loan staff to worthwhile projects or encourage employees to contribute "pro bono" skilled labor such as bookkeeping, legal representation or preparing public service ads. If your firm does not have such policies, work to convince them that community responsibility is an important part of good business practice.

Domestic Sullivan Principles

Several years ago the Rev. Leon Sullivan drew up what came to be known as the Sullivan Principles for corporations doing business in South Africa. The idea was that this objective set of standards could be used to determine whether or not a company was behaving responsibly by actions such as hiring and promoting people regardless of race. Though today most firms have come to believe that divestment is the only ethical course remaining in South Africa, the Sullivan Principles were an important beginning, establishing a bottom line of ethical responsibility in the midst of apartheid.

Hunger activist Nancy Amidei and a growing number of others are beginning to suggest that we need a similar list of principles for corporate behavior in our own country. It could include areas such as environmental impact, affirmative action in hiring disadvantaged people, benefits for employees, response to union organizing and other ways the corporation relates to its community and the world.

A key concern to raise in domestic "Sullivan Principles" is the problem of runaway shops: corporations moving factories to third world countries, where wages are low and regulations lax. Communities devastated by the human and social costs of plant closings want ways to hold corporate management responsible for keeping plants open or helping meet the costs of adjusting to the closing.

Agreement on and support for such principles is a long-term strategy, but we can begin preparing the groundwork and exchanging information with others doing similar work.

Many other ideas for individual responsibility suggested in chapter 15 can be extended to organizations as well. For example, your workplace or school can encourage people to car pool by providing ride boards or other ways to connect people with similar needs. Each of us can multiply our own growing sense of individual responsibility by working to extend it to the organizations that touch our lives.

Part Five

Share The Abundance

Dives didn't go to hell because he was rich. His wealth was an opportunity to bridge the gulf that separated him from his brother Lazarus. Dives went to hell because he passed by Lazarus every day, but he never really saw him. Dives went to hell because he wanted to be a conscientious objector in the war against poverty.

—Martin Luther King, Jr.

We're rich

We may not feel like we are, but anyone who can afford $7.95 for this book is most likely in the wealthier half of the world's population. As we think about the millions of people who will go to bed hungry tonight, we can stew in guilt, retreat into apathy or decide to share.

Some organizations deliberately provoke guilt feelings by flooding potential donors with pictures and heart-rending stories about hungry children. Such an approach may actually harm long-range efforts to help poor people become self-sufficient. It presents an image of hungry people as helpless and dependent, like children.

You can avoid the guilt trap. Emphasize success stories of those who have won power over their lives and resources and present positive images of those in need of help. Educate in a way that encourages people to get involved in a number of ways.

People are often reluctant to share generously because they fear that their gift will not be used responsibly. Most Americans view aid efforts with skepticism. We need to understand and share information about organizations that effectively help people overcome hunger and poverty if we are to give responsibly and encourage others to do likewise.

We must continue to encourage people to share with those in need. Although we Americans think of ourselves as compassionate, generous people, our per-person average contribution to efforts helping poor and hungry people is much lower than in most industrial nations. Nor are we any more generous than many poor people themselves who share their meager resources more often than we share from our abundance.

We often lack the habits and disciplines, the structures that systematically encourage us to remember the needs of others. A hunger bank on the family dining table, a designated day to bring canned goods for the food pantry to worship services or a well-publicized hunger walk gives people a needed reminder and a structured opportunity to live up to their ideals.

18

Raise Money

By Leslie Withers

Many people first get involved with world hunger by raising money to provide food for those who need it. While money is not the only solution, fundraising is part of the answer as well as an easy first step for many. Before beginning any fundraising project decide what organization or project will benefit. (See chapter 22 on how to evaluate an organization before giving money.) Meet with other people who share your concern to plan an appropriate project. (See chapter 1.)

The best fundraising projects are those that educate people, are fun and, of course, raise money. Here are some that other people have used.

Fasts And Special Meals

Many groups raise money for hunger causes with a fast or a special meal. Fasts are most effective in a school or other institution that serves regular meals. Organizers arrange with the cafeteria manager to skip the meal or prepare fewer servings and participants inform the food service of their pledge so they will have an accurate count. Then they attend a concert, program or discussion during the meal hour and donate the money saved to a designated hunger cause. Some also ask sponsors to contribute an amount based on the length of time the fast will last. Fasting for up to three days should not be harmful to a healthy adult, but children, elderly people, diabetics and those with health problems should not fast.

In another way to fast the group agrees to miss one meal a week, perhaps during a special season such as Lent, and contribute that money to hunger causes. The group may decide to meditate or pray together during the meal hour, or they may do that separately and later share their reflections. *Roots of Hope* is a collection of 52 miss-a-meal meditations published by *Seeds* and several denominations have published similar material. See the appendix for more information.

Hunger meals take many forms. (See chapter 19.) The easiest substitutes a simple meal for a more elaborate one: for example, beans and rice instead of a three course banquet. Charge the regular meal price, and contribute the money saved. But let the people know what to expect. The United Methodist Women in a Decatur, Georgia, church brought pots of soup and pans of cornbread made by members in place of the regular family night supper and raised $300 from 100 people who paid the regular price for the meal.

Everything-A-Thons

The hunger walk is the standard endurance contest to raise money for hunger. (See chapter 21.) The idea is to do an excessive amount of something and get sponsors to pay you to do it. It might be a walk-a-thon, bike-a-thon, canoe-a-thon, marathon or even a Jacuzzi-a-thon. (It happened. At an Arizona fraternity members took turns sitting in the jacuzzi for 72 hours while a frenzy of fundraising activities went on in the fraternity house.) Another growing movement on college campuses is the annual spring Hunger Cleanup. Students get sponsors to support them in spending a Saturday cleaning a public park, area of downtown or neighborhood, and the proceeds are given to a hunger cause.

Think big! Take a special event and expand it to something really special. Save our Cumberland Mountains (SOCM), a citizens organization fighting strip-mining in rural Tennessee, expanded a neighborhood walk-a-thon to transcontinental proportions. SOCM staffer Charles "Boomer" Winfrey canoed 1,800 miles for pledges. Although some pledges came from Washington, D.C. and New York City, most came from local people in the six Appalachian counties where they work. Each month pledgers received an eloquent account of Boomer's journey. The event captured the imagination of their supporters and most gifts were higher than average.

Product Sales

Kim Klein, co-publisher of the *Grassroots Fundraising Journal* says, "When you sell products, people can give to charity and get something they want in return." Church World Service and UNICEF raise money with sales of calendars and note cards, and so do many local hunger groups.

Enlist the help of local artists, photographers and graphic designers to promote your project. For both fundraising and educational purposes, positive images work better than negative ones. No one wants to be confronted by the wide eyes of a starving child every time they check their calendar.

Recipe books are another popular fundraiser. Some are simply collections of favorite recipes. Others concentrate on eating lower on the food chain, cooking for large groups, cooking with government surplus commodity foods, meals on a food stamp budget or recipes from an area where the group is also sponsoring a development project.

Product sales can be a spectacular way to lose money, too. Take a hard look at the potential market for your product before you invest money producing it. Draw up a marketing plan that includes potential buyers, how to reach them and a timeline. Estimate the product cost including staff time, the cost of publicity and shipping and/or handling. The sale cost of the product should be at least double the full cost of producing it, and many can return three or four times the cost. If double the cost is more than people would be willing to pay, the project is not realistic.

Consider product sales that make something out of nothing. The Metropolitan Opera in New York City sold vests and purses made from elegant collages of scraps from old costumes. Opera fans plunked down $80 for the men's vest and $90 for the women's vest made of costumes from "Aida" or "Boris Godunov." That musty stack of leftover T-shirts from the 1975 Hunger Walk might be this year's sentimental souvenir at twice the price.

Special Events

Use creative special events. Like products, they let people pay you for something they want. Adapt your traditional event to meet today's needs. CARE holds an annual "No-Show" banquet, with people buying tickets that entitle them to **not** attend and spare themselves the hassle of dressing up, driving across town and listening to boring speeches. Creative advertising donated by a large ad agency has made this non-event a major fundraiser.

The trick with special events is to be sure you have the audience before committing to the often-high expenses. Too many groups have lost money after hiring musicians, renting a hall, paying technicians and sending out announcements because of a disappointing turnout. If your group does not have a history or expertise with major events, proceed with caution.

Use the obvious interests and skills of your supporters: music, art, cooking. Creative thought can uncover other unusual fundraisers. In Baltimore a local dentist and 10 of his staff donated five hours of their time and services to benefit the Maryland Food Committee. They saw 23 patients and raised $1644. Hairdressers, portrait photographers, lawyers or auto mechanics could do the same.

Voluntary Tax

Do you love bananas but hate to buy them when you don't know whether Hondurans are getting fair pay? Do you favor buying locally grown produce but cringe and feed your coffee addiction? Follow the example of a Minnesota co-op grocery that carries these products but encourages its members to pay a voluntary tax on them. The tax can educate consumers about conditions under which the food is grown as well as raise money to support efforts for justice in oppressive situations.

Some families keep a hunger bank on the dining table and contribute at each meal. Presbyterians raise substantial amounts through a "two cents a meal" program that is promoted in many local churches. Families bring the money they have collected on a designated Sunday.

Many church groups use calendars that connect each day's giving with information about a particular country or situation. See the appendix for places to order hunger banks and calendars.

Raise Funds for Fundraisers

Raising money costs money as these examples make clear. Consider asking a foundation, church or other group to underwrite the cost of your fundraising project. Many will be attracted to the idea that investing $1000 will help the group raise $5000. Individuals, particularly board members and others strongly committed to the project or to the organization, may be willing to underwrite all or part of a particular project.

In-kind contributions can dramatically lower the cost of your fundraiser. With enough lead time and an attractive project you may find someone to give you almost everything you need from printing to T-shirts to food and drink. Ask the companies that make or distribute the products you need. (See chapter 3 for more fundraising ideas.)

19

Have a Hunger Meal

By Patricia Houck Sprinkle

Hunger meals provide excellent opportunities to raise hunger concerns. Before you decide to have one, however, decide why you want to have one. A hunger meal can raise money to fight hunger, or help people identify with hungry people. It can promote a simpler diet to conserve the world's resources; or help people experience the complexities and frustrations of the world's current food situation. Your goal may be any combination of these. What you want to achieve with your hunger meal determines the most effective meal to have.

Raise Money to Fight Hunger

This is probably the easiest goal to achieve, especially if your group meets regularly to eat at a mid-week dinner, for instance, or a monthly social. Set aside one meal, charge what you usually do, but either ask participants to fast for that meal or offer simpler fare: fruit, soup and cornbread or light sandwiches, fruit and milk. You can also raise money by charging for any of the other meals discussed below.

Identify with Hungry People

People who eat three meals a day do not experience the gnawing, numbing pangs that hungry people regularly know. To experience hunger even briefly, however, can stimulate a deeper concern and compassion.

Before this kind of meal ask participants to fast all day, if possible, and jot down their feelings as the day progresses. Ask them to bring their notes to the meal. Because rice is a staple in so much of the world, unseasoned brown rice and unsweetened tea is appropriate— one small bowl of rice and one cup of tea per person. Follow the meal with a discussion of how hunger affected each person and what effect it might have on a community or nation.

If you are considering America's hungry, serve a simple soup of mostly broth with a few vegetables, cornbread and fruit. You might want to find out what the welfare allotment is in your state, subtract the cost of housing and utilities, divide the rest to determine how much a person has for each meal, then spend that amount per person for food. Tell participants what the per meal allotment is. Some may want to try and live on that food budget for two weeks.

For a deeper experience, locate a soup kitchen in your area and either arrange to help serve a meal or to share a meal with those who come regularly. This provides first-hand contact with local people who are hungry. (Or follow another of the suggestions in chapter 5.)

Simpler, More Responsible Diet

Our standard diet consumes a large portion of the world's resources and damages our own health. If you wish to introduce your participants to the possibilities of not only eating but even enjoying simpler foods, make sure they get to taste some! (See chapters 15 and 17 for suggestions on the foods we eat.)

Your menu should contain little or no meat and should feature protein found in beans, rice and dairy products. You may want to introduce participants to soybeans or tofu. Good resources to help you prepare for this event are *The More With Less Cookbook* by Doris Janzen Longacre, *Great Meatless Meals* by Frances Moore Lappé, *Simply Delicious* by Grace Winn and *You've Got it Made: Make-Ahead Meals for the Family and for Cooperative Dinner Parties* by Marian Burros. These not only contain recipes, but Lappé and Longacre also provide information you can incorporate into placemats, wall posters and a program. See the appendix for more information.

You might stage the event in one of several ways:

● Have a buffet dinner and ask each cook to bring one low-meat or meatless casserole and a salad or a low-sugar dessert. Also, ask that each recipe be placed on a 3 x 5 card next to the dish and provide writing materials for those who want to copy it.

● Arrange participants at tables for four or eight and serve each table a different complete menu. Provide copies of menus and recipes and spoons for participants to graze at other tables when the meal is over.

● Set up a series of meals with a different menu and recipes for each one.

● If your group eats together regularly, designate each fourth meal a Less Meat or Meatless meal.

Simulate the World Food Situation

We who grew up with the privilege of three meals a day find it easy to forget that we were born here through no merit of our own and seldom consider that we may bear responsibility for those born elsewhere. What this type of simulation hopes to accomplish, therefore, is to let participants experience a microcosm of a world-wide meal in which most diners have little choice of what food or how much they eat. Events of this nature require more preparation but are highly effective in helping people understand more about world hunger through their own experience. To be effective the event must take participants by surprise, so keep your planning secret. Use a coffee break, a lunch or a whole dinner, and adjust your menu accordingly.

What you want to do is provide three different meals for the same group of people. Divide your guests into three groups. For each ten guests one represents the first world (Europe and USA); three represent the second world (Eastern Block); and six represent the third world. Prepare name tags and hand them out randomly, but be sure to maintain this ratio.

You may choose to let all diners sit together or designate areas of the room with crepe paper and show each person to his or her designated space. If using assigned spaces, be sure the first world group has flowers and that the third world group has too few chairs.

You may use a serving line, or serve guests in the designated eating areas. In either case, servers should distribute food according to the name tag. You may want to provide real china for first world guests, pottery dishes for the Eastern Block, and disposable dishes of the cheapest kind for third world guests.

Serve the first world group an elegant and lavish meal such as meat, rice and gravy, salad, vegetable, bread and butter, dessert and choice of beverage. Serve the Eastern Block rice and gravy, salad or vegetable, bread or dessert, beverage. Serve the third world group only a small portion of rice and water.

Permit the groups to eat for about 10 minutes, then make an announcement: "Persons with first world nametags, there's plenty of food in the kitchen, and you're entitled to all you want. Please come back for more." Be sure to stress they can get all they want but do not point out they can even get all they want to share. See if they figure it out.

Let group dynamics develop as they will. Some groups will share, others will squirm, some may even break into open hostilities! (Intervene only if you fear actual physical violence.)

The most important part of the meal is the discussion afterwards. Let persons from each of the three groups share what the meal meant for them.

How did they feel when they discovered what their tag meant?

How did they feel about their own group? The other two?

How did their own group deal with the situation? What are other ways they might have dealt with it?

How does this portray the world food situation?

How does it fall short?

One variation is to hand out vouchers which participants use to purchase their meal, giving each person some choice about menu. Be sure that the first world group receives enough vouchers to buy more than everything on the menu, the Eastern Block group receives enough to buy about half the menu items, and the third world group receives only enough to purchase rice and half of one other item.

A Meal Is More than Food.

The decor of your eating space can enhance the educational experience. Decorate the room with posters, slogans and/or scripture verses pertaining to hunger or justice. Print or purchase placemats with hunger quizzes, scripture verses or hunger facts. Simple illustrations that children can take home and color can be used on place mats also. If you are raising money with the event, provide materials to show where the money will go. You may want to show a film or have a speaker after your meal.

All of these meals will leave diners with feelings and a learning experience they may want and need to share. Be sure to provide a time for participants to talk in small groups or as a whole. Ask for ideas on how the group might get further involved with the problem of hunger. You may want to close with a time of commitment or prayer for hungry people around the world.

20

Grow, Collect and Scrounge

*By Susan McCarter, Leslie Withers,
and Jan Buckingham*

Raising money can help hungry people, but why not raise food? Or collect surplus food—particularly food that would be wasted? Investing muscle and sweat instead of writing a check can increase people's commitment as well as their understanding of the food chain on which we all depend.

Across the country food drives, harvest festivals, cooperative gardens and gleaning from commercial farms and orchards make more food available to hungry people. Although food banks and food pantries provide nutritious food from which well-rounded meals can be prepared, fresh fruit and vegetables are seldom available. Harvest festivals, cooperative gardens and gleaning can fill the gap.

Before you begin remember that the most efficient way to get nutritious food to people who need it is to raise money to buy food in wholesale lots and/or from your local food bank. Growing, harvesting and collecting food is labor-intensive work that requires a tight schedule and the ability to transport and store large quantities of perishables.

Cooperative Gardens

Cooperative gardens can be as varied as the people who grow them. A church or synagogue with spacious grounds could have its garden on its property. Few sights are as beautiful as healthy vegetables interspersed with marigolds and other insect-repelling flowers. Vegetables and fruit can be interplanted in and around the foundation. Parsley and chives make beautiful border plants, and strawberries planted in a foot-wide row around the property are always an appealing sight.

An inner-city group with little land might rent a nearby vacant lot. Some cities set aside land for community gardens. Utility companies may make power line rights-of-way available. Senior Citizen centers, youth clubs and schools have potential garden sites as well.

Some gardens are subdivided into separate plots that are planted, tended and harvested by individuals and families. Others encourage members to work cooperatively and send produce to needy families, a local soup kitchen or food bank. One church terraced the hill behind its building and provided more than 1,000 pounds of greens a year for a downtown soup kitchen. Another alternative is to sell the food on Saturday mornings and use the proceeds to feed hungry people.

A group of churches in Waco, Texas, gardens cooperatively. Each church concentrates on one vegetable: one church grows potatoes, another beans, another tomatoes. With each church focused on its specialty they provide larger quantities of food.

Be clear about who bears responsibility for the garden: the church committee, a gardening club at the Senior Center or an independent organization. (See chapter 1 for suggestions on starting and maintaining a group.) Decisions to be made include choosing a garden site (Availability of water will influence choice.); what will be done with the produce; what sort of participation is expected; and who will take on tasks such as hauling the produce to the food bank. Decide whether plots will be assigned to individuals and families or whether the whole garden will be a cooperative venture. Consider cooperative purchasing of seeds, tools, fertilizer, lime and gardening books. Should the garden be hand-dug, or should a rototiller be rented? Will the garden be organic or will chemicals be used? Your local county agricultural extension service will probably be able to give advice and practical help even if you live in a city.

Cooperative gardening can be one of the most enjoyable and productive projects your group has ever tackled. Beginners can learn from more experienced gardeners, and people of widely different ages and backgrounds can enjoy the fellowship and the satisfaction of achieving concrete, measurable results.

For ongoing information from other community gardeners, subscribe to *The Journal of Community Gardening*. (See appendix for details.)

Supermarket Food Drives

A supermarket food drive is an effective way to collect canned and nonperishable foods for the emergency pantry or food bank. People entering the store are invited to buy items to donate as they leave. Choose a popular store where many people do their shopping. Supermarkets located in malls where you won't have to worry about busy street traffic can be particularly good sites. If the store has more than one entrance, cover each door. Try to have at least two people at each entrance, so they can support each other while soliciting food.

To set up a grocery store food drive, first prepare yourself with information about the pantry or food bank you are assisting. You will need to know its distribution policies and the number of people helped when you ask for donations of food or time. Also, find out what kind of food they need so you can guide contributions.

Next, consult in person with the store manager. Tell him or her what the food drive is for and request your first choice of date and time. Friday evenings through Saturday evenings are generally best since most stores are busiest then. Select more than one date so the store manager will have a choice. Be flexible and assure the manager that you will keep the collection drive quiet and nondisruptive. Emphasize that civic-minded shoppers will spend more money in the supermarket to contribute to the drive. Assure the manager that you will clean up afterward.

While a few people can collect a sizable amount of food at one store with a minimum of organizing, some groups plan for a community-wide drive, with collection points in many stores. For a large-scale food drive, once you have a date and time, enlist other agencies and organizations to help with publicity and supervision of the collection sites. Issue a letter of invitation at least three weeks before the drive, including:

● Full name, address and telephone number of your organization;

● A brief summary of your group's goals and achievements to serve as an introduction to your organization;

● The time and place of your food drive; where the food is to be used and by whom;

● An explanation of how each organization can help in the food drive.

Send a news release to local newspapers and a public service announcement to local radio and television stations. (See chapter 24 for tips on working with media.) Attractive posters and flyers in the store and the surrounding community are helpful, too.

After the drive remember to send thank-you letters to the supermarket manager and to individuals and organizations that helped.

Other Food Drives

The simplest, most common food drive occurs in hundreds of churches and synagogues every week. On a designated date people bring contributions of canned and staple foods to place in a box at the door or bring forward during the service. Frequently congregations continue the drive for a month to give everyone an opportunity to participate. Check ahead with the pantry or food bank using the food to find out what they need and publicize that information through the church newsletter, bulletin or announcements.

Donations of food can also be part of the price of admission to a concert, hunger walk or other public event.

Some groups invite gardeners to bring surplus produce to gatherings during harvest season and either contribute it to the food bank or sell it to other church members and donate the proceeds to hunger causes. Integrating a "harvest festival" into a worship service can be the occasion to remember both God's bounty and the needs of hungry people.

Gleaning

Gleaning is the practice of gathering food left behind in the fields after harvest. Historically, gleaning was a source of food for the poor, but modern living has isolated the urban poor from food production both culturally and geographically. Meanwhile, modern harvesting, market fluctuations and demand for standardized produce waste up to one-fifth of the American harvest: 137 millions tons and billions of dollars worth every year. Organized gleaning is one way this waste can translate into food for people whose income doesn't cover their basic needs.

If your group wants to experiment with gleaning, you will need to negotiate with one or more farmers and be prepared to go to the fields with volunteers and a large enough truck to transport what you gather. Volunteers will need tools and containers for their work as well as water, snacks and first aid equipment. You will also need to arrange ahead with the food bank or pantry to make sure they will be able to store and use what you gather.

Keep accurate records. You'll need them for the IRS, so farmers can get a tax deduction for their donation. Good records will also make the second year's gleaning program easier and more successful. Large ongoing gleaning projects keep computer lists of farmers who donate and amounts harvested. They have crop watchers and also send reminders to former donors to insure the largest possible harvest and to keep a mutually beneficial relationship with the farmers.

Farmers may be reluctant to permit gleaning for several reasons. One major problem—liability—has been solved in many states by "Good Samaritan" laws that absolve farmers from liability. Or volunteers can sign a waiver or take out liability insurance. Farmers concerned that handouts will go to able-bodied people need to know that the gleaners are connected to food banks or other non-profit organizations that assure produce is given—not sold—to those in need.

Foremost, farmers are in business, and volunteers must be trained as harvesters so the fields or orchards will not be damaged. Be careful not to interfere with farmers' work schedules. For example, Project Glean once got a call to harvest a field of melons in Brentwood, California. The farmer was discing the field, and the crew worked just ahead of him as fast as they could. Although they harvested 26,000 pounds of melons, they didn't finish. By the next day the whole field was plowed under.

Once the food is harvested you'll need a place to sort and clean what you've gleaned—perhaps the same food bank or pantry that will distribute it. Arrange for the gleaners or another group of volunteers to do this task, so your donation does not become a burden to the group receiving the food. You may also need to package and store some food.

The next step beyond gleaning itself can be preserving food for leaner seasons. Project Glean harvested 20,000 pounds of apricots in three weeks and 31,000 pounds of pears in a month. They offer any group who wants to dry fruit the use of their dehydrators and arrange for the cooperative extension agent to teach canning and freezing techniques.

You will need plenty of volunteers to keep the program going since labor intensive gleaning would not otherwise be an economic way of providing food for needy people. Many will be senior citizens with free time during the day. Reach out beyond your traditional volunteers to include refugees, young people, the mentally disabled—all will gain a sense of community from their efforts.

In a large, highly organized project, gleaners may sign up for at least eight hours of work per month, pay a $10 fee and be entitled to 25 percent of what they glean. We may think of gleaning as altruistic, but many will participate for the food.

An Idaho gleaning organization gives special emphasis to self-help and to helping others. Most of the gleaners are young mothers, many single, who couldn't feed their families without food gleaned from backyards and farms. Each gleaner has a "silent partner," one or more persons who are unable to pick for themselves. Since the Idaho harvesting season is short, the silent partner sometimes helps in canning and freezing, but often the food is simply given to disabled and elderly partners.

Gleaning in Idaho includes excess fish from fish hatcheries as well as hunters' donations and illegal game kills—elk, moose, antelope and even bear. Any food that might be wasted in the community is given to the group, from unsold grocers' stock to a 4-H student's livestock project.

Harvest of Hope, a ministry of the Society of St. Andrew in Virginia, has given away millions of pounds of potatoes. Their program combines intense study with the hard physical work of harvesting. Young people or adults live together for a week, and learn about community and world hunger. Each day after leaving the fields they examine world hunger through Bible study, simulations, audio-visuals, games, discussion and worship. For many it is not just a one-week adventure but the beginning of a lifetime commitment.

Several groups with a history of successful gleaning are willing to answer questions and provide information to new groups. Check the appendix for the address and phone number of Project Glean, the Idaho Hunger Action Council and Harvest of Hope.

According to George Keenen of Food Share in Oxnard, California, gleaning is a win, win, win situation. The poor get food that doesn't cost anything and, therefore, increase their purchasing power; the donor usually gets a tax break and waste is reduced.

Have a Hunger Walk

By Leslie Withers

More than 2,000 U.S. communities annually hold hunger walks, ranging from 30 walkers on North Carolina's Outer Banks to 25,000 in Boston. Varying in age, background, faith, race and political persuasion, the walkers are united by their desire to feed hungry people. Money is raised as sponsors contribute a certain amount per mile or kilometer that the walker completes. Church World Service, which organizes 1,800 CROP walks each year, says the average walker raises $30.

Communities distribute the money in different ways. For example, in CROP walks, 75 percent of the money collected goes to an international agency chosen by the sponsor from a list approved by Church World Service. The rest is given locally. Half the money raised in Louisville supports their food bank and the other half goes to a different overseas project each year. Boston's Project Bread has organized a walk for 18 years and is the primary funding source for 200 local food programs. They also give 10 percent of the money raised to designated overseas agencies. The more than $2 million raised in 1986 makes this the country's largest walk.

More than a fund raiser, a walk is a way to show people they don't have to accept hunger or feel guilty. They can work together on solutions. For many, a walk is their first active involvement around hunger. Walkers meet other concerned people and are introduced to hunger organizations in their community. Many then go on to volunteer in a food bank, join Bread for the World or otherwise "take the next step."

Starting a Hunger Walk

First, find other people to work with. (See chapter 1 on how to start a group.) Most walks involve churches and/or hunger organizations. Local soup kitchens and food banks can be helpful, but be careful not to compete with them for community resources.

If you are considering a CROP walk, Church World Service (CWS) has organized walks since the 1950s and has an excellent step-by-step manual. Printed materials for your walk are free, and regional staff give help and advice. CWS also furnishes educational resources, films and slide shows to anyone whether for a CROP walk or not. The free 20-minute film, "A Spirit of Celebration," is a great way to get people excited about walking. (See appendix for address.)

Begin by coming to a common understanding of why you're doing the walk. Set goals: number of participating organizations, number of walkers, amount of money to be raised. Do not set unrealistic goals, particularly if it's your first walk. Remember that numbers and dollars are not your only goals. Start planning early; plans for an October walk (to coincide with World Food Day) should begin in the spring. Some walks are held on Saturday, others on Sunday afternoon.

Other early decisions to make include:
● The name of the group and the name of the walk
● How to establish credibility for the walk (sponsors, an advisory board of prominent people)
● Where the money raised will go
● Who will chair or co-chair and who will act as treasurer
● Necessary task forces or committees and who will chair them
● The time and starting point of the walk. (Most people's experience has been that it's better to hold the walk, rain or shine, than to set a rain date.)

Once basic decisions are made and the committees set up, the entire group won't need to meet often. Nothing kills enthusiasm faster than endless meetings! Most of the real work will be done in the committees and the committee chairs can serve as a steering committee to coordinate the work and make remaining decisions.

Money

Determine the criteria for which organizations will receive funds. Most groups decide that at least some money should go to local efforts. Often a portion is given to international efforts or widely-known organizations that inspire enthusiastic support. Sometimes money is allocated to educational and advocacy groups as well as to feeding people. These decisions should be made before you print materials about the walk. They will influence who will be willing to work on the walk, sponsor it and participate in it.

Financial procedures need to be set and clearly stated. For a small walk the treasurer can handle the finances, but larger walks call for a finance committee. (See below.) You may need to incorporate as a tax-exempt organization, but don't unless you have to. It's time consuming and often expensive. Perhaps an already existing tax-exempt organization will receive and disburse money for the walk.

Decide on a budget and how to cover costs. Boston's Project Bread pays a modest overhead of about 16 percent for its small staff and other expenses. In Louisville the 13 sponsoring groups rotate responsibility for covering costs which run around $900. Other walks divide expenses among sponsoring organizations or set up a fund raising committee. Start early to line up sponsors for donated printing, legal help, paper cups, balloons, a telephone answering machine, office space and other services.

Working Committees

You will probably need recruitment, arrangements and publicity committees. Consider also committees for education, finance, refreshments and registration. Each group needs a chair (or co-chairs) and a representative to the steering committee, who may or may not be the same person. Someone needs to keep minutes which can be circulated to committee members and to chairs of the other committees. A timeline that also states who is responsible for each task is essential.

The recruitment committee has the largest job and needs the most members and longest lead time. Its goal is to find a walk coordinator within each church, club, school, business or other institution whose members are potential walkers. The committee should hold one or more workshops for the coordinators, make sure they get the information and materials they need and stay in touch with them after the walk until all funds have been turned in.

Walk coordinators publicize the walk, recruit walkers, give them the materials they need to enlist sponsors and collect and turn in the money. The recruiters' workshop equips them for this. In a church, for example, the coordinator might place announcements in the bulletin and church newsletter, put up posters and attend various meetings to explain the walk and sign up walkers. She or he could also arrange for a film or speaker a week or two before the walk. A hunger emphasis for the the church could be set up for the period of time leading up to the walk.

The publicity committee promotes the walk, primarily through the news media. (See chapter 24 on working with media.) Since their work determines how the public views the walk, their major decisions about spokespeople, slogans and information to be emphasized should be approved by the steering committee. Once the concepts are agreed upon, they design and produce posters or flyers and circulate public service announcements to newspapers, radio and TV stations. Then send out press releases ahead of the walk, on the day of the walk, and afterward that tell how much money was raised and what groups received it.

If contacted well in advance (preferably by a prominent person) a public relations firm may agree to sponsor your walk. They can be tremendously helpful in creating promotional materials and drawing media attention. Radio and television stations and newspapers also sponsor hunger walks.

Decide whether the publicity committee will also take on internal communications such as producing packets or posters for recruiters, or whether another group will do this. CWS provides much of this material for CROP walks, but for others this can be a time-consuming and potentially expensive task.

The arrangements committee sets up the walk route. With clearly defined start and finish lines to avoid car problems, most find it easiest to begin and end the walk at the same place. A ribbon to cut or balloons to release at the start provide a festive official beginning. The committee makes sure the route is safe and well-marked and provides water, refreshments and restrooms, arranges for loudspeaker systems, gets necessary permits, etc. They should contact groups that hold marathons or other walks for advice and help with equipment such as walkie talkies, pylons and safety vests for traffic monitors. Your police department can help with safety and can minimize traffic tie-ups. Some walks purchase accident insurance while others require walkers to sign liability waivers.

Decide whether the arrangements committee or another group will register walkers and hand out certificates, T-shirts or other awards to those completing the route. Some longer walks validate walkers' tickets as they pass key points.

The finance committee sets up procedures for collecting and disbursing funds and keeps financial records. If you anticipate a large number of walkers, deposit slips can be given to each walk coordinator to deposit money as they collect it. They send a copy of each deposit slip with a form that tells where the money came from and gives other necessary information. Set deadlines for receipt of money. Remind people often of the deadline.

Since most of this committee's work comes after the event, it might also work ahead of the walk to raise money for walk expenses.

The education committee makes the walk a learning event by arranging displays from hunger groups at the walk, a speakers bureau or film list for groups to use before the walk and arranging for bands, clowns and entertainment. Walks can include rest stops in churches that feed and shelter people, routes that bring walkers face-to-face with poverty, a lunch stop with music and speakers, opportunities to join organizations and tables where people can write letters to federal or local officials.

If you have a send-off ceremony at the beginning, *keep it short!* People came to walk not to listen to speeches. Five minutes from a prominent person like the mayor, a few last-minute reminders by a walk organizer and perhaps an invocation by a local minister are as much as you need.

Some Helpful Hints
● Decentralize. Don't let the walk become identified with one church, one person or one organization. Work for the broadest possible ownership and involvement.
● Start in plenty of time. Allow eight weeks to plan and prepare for a modest walk in a small community—more time in a larger city.
● Invest most of the group's time and energy in recruitment. Recruit

people one-on-one, through churches and organizations, with posters and public service announcements. Involve local "celebrities" and public officials. Perhaps the mayor will issue a proclamation or declare a special Hunger Walk Day.

• Have aggressive follow-up to get the money in quickly after the walk.
• Have clear, easily understood, responsible procedures for collecting and distributing funds. Publish a report after the walk that states how much was collected and where it went.
• Be sure to have adequate water and first aid along the walk route.
• Don't set your sights too high, especially for a first walk. Celebrate, have a good time, enjoy and appreciate the folks who show up.
• Keep expenses to a bare minimum. You'll find with a bit of legwork that most of what you need can be donated.

Improving an Existing Hunger Walk

If your area already has a hunger walk, work to improve it. Set a date for an evaluation about two weeks after the walk. Invite anyone who helped put on the walk. Discuss what went well and why and what did not go well and how to avoid those problems next year. Have an evaluation form for those who can't come to the meeting. Take good notes, and be sure the organizers of next year's walk have copies.

Keep finding more walkers every year by strengthening the recruitment and the publicity committees. Challenge each walker to raise more money as well. Set goals for recruiters, publicize the total goal and encourage walkers to set their own.

Consider a development committee to: look for "important people" to endorse and participate in the walk; line up a public relations firm and a radio station to officially sponsor the walk; and seek corporate and church funding for walk expenses. This group can also look for donated office space and other "in-kind" contributions.

Ed King, who coordinates CROP walks in the Carolinas, points to another direction for enlarging and improving hunger walks. "We must not be satisfied with the present successful athletic marathons and money raised no matter how many miles walked or per-walker dollars collected for charity. We should also use our walks to raise awareness and support other closely related justice-fighters presently isolated or neglected and without a support system. We can celebrate their causes and make them our own by networking with them, evolving our CROP walks into larger annual Shalom Festivals.

"Everyone loves a parade," says King. "Something magic happens when people join hands in the street to celebrate their lives, their concerns for others, their music, their color, their poster art and other creative talents. Diversity, networking and pluralism in the walk are community strengths. As we learn more about global interdependence and the many complex, related root causes and effects of local and global hunger, we will reflect that deeper understanding and knowledge in our walks."

22

Give Money Responsibly

By Louis L. Knowles

Giving money is the first and easiest way for many people to become involved in hunger work. Clearly, sharing our resources with those in need is a compassionate and responsible act. We are often blocked from taking this step because we don't know if our resources will be well used by the particular group asking us for money.

A simple answer for many is to give through their church or denomination. Most denominations have a long, proven history of effective and compassionate work among hungry people. Because the overhead (buildings, staff, etc.) is often subsidized by the overall church structure, a higher percentage of designated funds can go directly into hunger work. Many other organizations also do good work and deserve our support.

These organizations provide channels for effective action to end hunger in three areas: relief in crisis, support for development, and education and political action. Since each kind of work is important, people of conscience should seek out efficient and effective organizations.

What You Should Know About Hunger Organizations

Before giving a substantial amount of money to any organization you're not well acquainted with, find out if the money is well used. As an educated donor of a large sum, you should be encouraged to participate in the life of the organization and take advantage of printed materials and learning opportunities that usually accompany donations over $100.

Checking the organization's latest annual report and audited financial statement will answer many important questions. If an organization is advertising on television, these documents may be obtained by calling the toll-free number. Independent opinions can be obtained from denominational or ecumenical staff of hunger ministries. A responsible donor will need the following information.

The Stated Purpose of the Organization

A statement of purpose tells a great deal about an organization. It

118

tells whether it is denominational, ecumenical or secular. It defines goals and indicates special interests such as health care, children's welfare or food aid. Look carefully to see if the purpose is well-defined or general and murky.

Activities of the Organization
The key to the philosophy of the group is whether it stresses relief, development, education or political action. Most organizations specialize in one or two.

Leadership
You should know who serves on the board of directors. Although directors are usually not deeply engaged in the day-to-day work of an organization, their professional and political experience gives important clues to the general direction of the agency. The board should have a balance of professional development workers and business executives. Women and minorities should be included on the board as well as people from poor countries. The background of the executive director is important.

Maintain Ties with Third World People
Agencies that respond to crises and foster development in poor countries fall roughly into three categories: those that maintain official relations with third world governments and work through government agencies; those that work primarily through churches and ecumenical committees in third world countries; and those that relate to religious and secular, and governmental and non-governmental agencies.

All have something to contribute but some will be more effective in certain situations than others. For example, an agency that works through the government of a local country will probably be more successful in helping people if the government is democratic and non-repressive. On the other hand, an agency that relates to church committees or to local peasant movements may be particularly helpful in a country where the government is a cause of poverty.

Some agencies build networks of committees that depend on the "parent" organization for purpose and support while others seek existing community organizations and grassroots movements and offer their assistance. In the first case, the agency has more control over its programs but sacrifices local initiative. In the second case, the hunger agency has less control but participation by local community leaders is greater.

Sources of Money
Organizations generally obtain funds for overseas work from U.S. government sources, churches and other private sources, or some of each.

An agency that receives a large amount of money from the U.S. government will naturally pay close attention to U.S. foreign policy concerns. This may limit the work, but government funds usually provide the organization with far more resources than could be raised otherwise. At the other end of the spectrum, organizations that receive little or no money from the government are not restricted by foreign policy considerations but must work harder to raise funds. They, however, are often much smaller and must be sensitive to the interests and preferences of their own donors.

How the Funds are Used

It is important to know how much of the donation is applied to problems of world hunger. Inevitably, some funds must pay for management and fundraising costs—generally, 20 percent or less. Finding the percentage and comparing it among organizations may be difficult since financial reporting methods vary from group to group. A financial statement usually provides a general picture of overhead costs. If some categories sound vague or ill-defined, the donor may need to seek more information to determine if some overhead is hidden.

No absolute rule defines how much should be spent on administration and fundraising. Smaller organizations have a harder time keeping costs down since larger groups benefit from economies of scale. Groups that handle large amounts of U.S. government food aid are able to keep overall management cost down to a very small part of the total budget. On the other hand, organizations that specialize in lobbying or education will spend high portions of their budget on staff salaries. A casual glance might suggest overhead is much too high, but your contribution pays for expertise, instruction and coordination for effectively addressing hunger concerns.

Deciding on Projects

Virtually all organizations claim that project ideas originate from those being served and important program decisions are made at the grass-roots level. Without on-site inspection of a project in a developing country, determining who actually makes decisions may be impossible, but the question is still important. A committee generally makes final go-ahead decisions on funding. Knowing the composition of this group can help to determine who is really calling the shots.

Evaluation

Despite the hundreds of millions of dollars spent every year by world hunger organizations, program evaluation remains at a primitive stage. Third-party evaluation of projects is rare. Evaluation practices vary considerably, but most are still in the formative stages.

The U.S. government is one of the few groups doing substantial independent evaluation of world hunger organizations. USAID wants to know what really happens to the hundreds of millions of dollars it grants to organizations for relief and development projects. Recently the General Accounting Office evaluated several private voluntary organizations' development projects in order to give AID guidance. Results show unevenness in agency performance. Good and bad development projects often exist within the same organization.

The National Charities Information Bureau (NCIB) is an independent watchdog organization that helps keep philanthropies true to the ideals and standards that should characterize all charitable organizations. NCIB publishes a monthly list called the "Wise Giving Guide," which lists dozens of organizations and indicates whether or not they meet NCIB's criteria. NCIB also publishes reports about each organization on its list which are available to the public. Individuals who contribute $25.00 to NCIB will receive the "Wise Giving Guide" for a year and may request any number of reports by phone or mail. Single copies of "Wise Giving Guide" and up to three individual organizational reports are available free on a one-time-only basis to nonmembers. See the Appendix for the address and phone number. Keep in mind that the NCIB is primarily a financial watchdog and does not evaluate the organization's philosophy or quality of work. It does look at the board of directors and does not approve organizations with more than one staff person as a voting member of the board.

The Philanthropic Advisory Service of the Council of Better Business Bureau provides information about organizations that solicit funds, including world hunger organizations. The Service publishes a bimonthly list of the organizations that have generated the greatest number of inquiries in recent weeks. The list indicates which organizations meet their criteria and is available to the public for $1.00 and a self-addressed, stamped envelope. See their listing in the Appendix.

For most donors the audited financial statement of an organization and a report from the National Charities Information Bureau will answer any questions. For someone interested in checking every possible source of information reports are available for most charitable organizations from the Internal Revenue Service and the governments of the states of New York and California.

Eight questions to ask:

1. What is the purpose of the organization?
2. What type of action does it engage in?
3. Who is in charge? Who is on the Board of Directors?
4. How does the group maintain ties with people in the third world?
5. Where does the money come from?
6. Where does the money go?
7. Who decides which projects to pursue?
8. How are the projects evaluated?

Part Six

Spread The Word

If you are thinking a year ahead, sow seed. If you are thinking ten years ahead, plant a tree. If you are thinking one hundred years ahead, educate the people.

—Chinese Poet, 500 B.C.

How many new people attended the last hunger task force meeting? Are the people who chaired this year's hunger walk the same people who chaired last year's? Do you know everyone in your community who is working against hunger? Is burnout a problem? Take a look at your outreach. An organization that doesn't have new folks at each meeting isn't a movement—it's a support group. While we all need support, hungry people need a movement.

To build a movement we have to encourage new people and new organizations to become involved while we continue to nurture each other. We need to build ongoing education and opportunities for involvement into our congregations, schools and service organizations. We must reach out to the general public through the news media.

Churches and synagogues provide much of the people-power and financial support for work against hunger and poverty. This shouldn't be surprising since they have both a scriptural mandate to care for poor people and structured ways to respond. Congregations can also be fertile ground for outreach: Even the most active congregation can rely on a few key people or assume everyone understands what some have learned. Other congregations have barely begun to tap the potential pool of money and energy available among their members.

Outreach should take us to some unexpected places as well as to the people or organizations that we expect to care about hunger and poverty. Local professional associations, civic clubs, schools, neighborhood organizations or local garden clubs all regularly look for programs and speakers. Besides information on the particular topic, we can offer them opportunities to get involved, and we can come away with names and phone numbers of those who want to do something.

Educate Your Congregation

By Leslie Withers

Ministers of Education, Sunday school leaders or members of a hunger task force, who are responsible for the ongoing education of their congregation, need to work to continually keep hunger concerns in front of their congregations and help them act effectively. (If your congregation does not already have a hunger task force, see chapter 1.) "Education" includes not only classroom activities but also other opportunities to learn, including worship, holiday observances and mealtimes.

Study Scripture
For Christians and Jews, our common scriptures provide many insights into current problems of poverty and hunger as well as God's promise of *shalom*—wholeness, reconciliation and abundance for all God's children.

God's particular love and concern for poor and hungry people and the call for justice resound through every book of scripture but are often overlooked. Poor translations, inadequate teaching or our desire to find comfort and justification are reasons for the oversight. A careful examination into scripture shows people are hungry because they're poor and poor because they're oppressed.

Hebrew, the original language of the Torah, Talmud, and Old Testament, has 15 different root words for "oppress" and "oppression" which appear more than 300 times in scripture. Search through a concordance or another guide for words in scripture like oppress, oppression, poor, and poverty. Compare several different translations for key passages.

Scriptures common to Christians and Jews contain significant teaching about hunger, poverty and justice in the accounts of the creation and stewardship, the Exodus and liberation and in the prophets. One plan for a study program might look like this:

First Session: Search for poverty and oppression in scripture, and give an overview of following session.
Second Session: Study creation and stewardship in Genesis. God

creates a bountiful world, and we are to manage it for the good of all.

Third and Fourth Sessions: In the Exodus event God liberates the Hebrew people from oppression, makes a covenant with them and shows them how to live together in the promised land "flowing with milk and honey."

Fifth and Sixth Sessions: The prophets expose the nation's fall away from justice into divisions of wealth and poverty marked by exploitation of the weak and the poor. But the prophets also hold up the vision of *shalom*—God's promise of justice and plenty for all who keep the covenants.

Subsequent sessions in Christian churches could deal with Jesus' teachings and with the actions of the early church. See the appendix for listings of helpful materials for Bible study.

Incorporating the "Real" World

Scripture becomes meaningful when people connect what the Bible teaches with their own lives and world. A good study plan includes ways for people to experience and reflect on the world we live in as well as scriptural teaching. Bread for the World has single lesson plans and two excellent study courses. (See the appendix for more information.) Your denomination may have such material as well.

The best plan of study will give class members experience with poor people as well as written material and will lead them toward further involvement. This is not easy, since many of us seldom see or know a poor person. If your congregation does not already have direct involvement with hungry people, you may need to find other ways to encounter the realities of poverty. (See chapter 4.) A study group combined with a community survey would add down-to-earth reality to your studies. (See chapter 6.)

Worship

The worship service offers the whole congregation a chance to reflect on God's will for our individual lives and the world we live in. Hunger and poverty, oppression and the need for justice permeate both scripture and the world. Hunger should be an ongoing concern for every community of faith not just a topic once a year. Worship should complement the education and service work of the congregation. Sermons, liturgy and music can regularly call us to faithfulness and commitment by recounting God's goodness and bounty. Beware of guilt-laden approaches that leave people feeling helpless in the face of overwhelming problems.

Special Seasons

"Every time you plan lessons and activities for a holiday, include a component about feeding the hungry. Some holidays lend themselves

125

to this more easily than others, but each one can provoke thought and action on the problem of hunger, keeping the issue in front of the congregation all year." (*Feed the World: a Crisis Curriculum*, prepared by the Coalition for Alternatives in Jewish Education.) For Jews, this particular curriculum suggests innovative ways to integrate hunger concerns into observances of Rosh Hashanah, Yom Kippur, Sukkot, Simchat Torah, Chanukah, Tu B'Shevat, Purim, and Pesach.

For Christians, Advent, Christmas and Epiphany offer chances for alternative celebrations that don't focus on selfishness and greed but on charity and justice. The 40 days of Lent could be a time to reflect on our relationship to the poor. Recalling both the 40 days when Jesus fasted in the wilderness and the 40 years that the Hebrew children wandered the wilderness dependent on God for the daily manna, Lent can call us to simplicity, to repentence and to greater willingness to risk our own security in the service of others. The long Pentecost season leads from inward reflection and personal salvation to the call of the Spirit to go out into all the world with good news.

Education Involves More Than Words
Work to bring your congregation's actions in line with its teachings. For example, a church budget that funds a "family life center" and doesn't support a food pantry speaks more loudly than a year's sermons on "world hunger." (See chapter 4 for other suggestions.)

Remember, hunger and poverty are not intellectual problems. They affect those who suffer and those who observe on deep spiritual and emotional levels. Learning, therefore, needs to involve our bodies and emotions as well as our minds. Young people may learn more from a simulation game than from weeks in a classroom. Don't make the unfortunate mistake of thinking that games and songs, dramas and drawings, are only for kids. Hunger workshops for adults become powerful, life-changing events when the resource team includes not only "hunger experts" but also people with skills in drama, liturgy and music. As participants work to express what they're learning intellectually with their bodies and emotions, new insights and ideas emerge and the group's energy increases.

Each of us needs to continue to learn, and a congregation with normal turnover in membership needs to find ways for new people to learn what others already know. The educator's job is never finished.

Biblical Passages Related to Hunger and Justice

Genesis 1:29-30 . . . . . . *God gives the world's food to Adam and Eve*
Exodus 3:7-12 . . . . *Moses asked to go to Pharoah*
Exodus 16:1-36 . . . . *the manna lifestyle*
Leviticus 19:9-11 . . . . . . *leave a portion of your harvest for the poor*
Numbers 11:4-6 . . . . *people greedy for meat*
Deuteronomy 14:28-15:11 . *a redistribution of wealth; a law of tithe*

1 Kings 21:1-20 .... *lust for land leads to deceit and oppression*
Psalm 72:1-14 .... *how to pray for government*
Psalm 82:1-4 .... *justice to the weak and destitute*
Psalm 146:5-9 .... *the Lord is just and feeds the hungry*
Proverbs 14:21 .... *happy are they who are kind to the poor*
Proverbs 19:17 .... *who is kind to the poor lends to the Lord*
Proverbs 21:13 .... *listen to the cry of the poor*
Isaiah 1:17 .... *seek justice—correct oppression*
Isaiah 3:14-15 .... *Why do you grind the face of the poor?*
Isaiah 5:1-7 .... *I looked for justice but beheld bloodshed*
Isaiah 58:6-12 .... *pour yourself out for the hungry*
Jeremiah 22:13-16 .... *to know the Lord is to do justice*
Ezekiel 16:49-50 .. *Sodom destroyed because of neglect of the poor*
Amos 4:1-3 ...... *elite and wealthy women implicated in injustice*
Amos 5:10-24 .... *let justice roll down like waters*
Amos 8:4-7 .... *the greedy buy the poor for silver*
Micah 6:8 .... *do justice, love mercy, walk humbly*
Matthew 5:23-24 .... *first be reconciled, then offer your gifts*
Matthew 6:25-34 .... *seek the kingdom of God and justice first*
Matthew 23:23 .... *you have neglected justice, mercy and faith*
Matthew 25:31-46 .... *I was hungry and you gave me food*
Mark 8:1-9 .... *feeding the multitude, also John 6:1-14*
Luke 1:46-55 .... *Mary's magnificat*
Luke 10:25-37 .... *good samaritan*
Luke 14:12-14 .... *invite the poor to your dinner*
Luke 16:19-31 .... *rich man and Lazarus*
Luke 19:1-9 .... *Zacchaeus' radical generosity*
John 6:25-35, 47-51 .... *I am the bread of life*
John 13:3-15 .... *Jesus washing the disciples' feet*
Acts 2:42-47, 32-35 .... *sharing in the early church*
Acts 6:1-6 .... *first dispute in church over distribution of food*
I Corinthians 11:17-34 ..... *selfishness in the Christian assembly*
I Corinthians 16:1-2 .... *put aside for the needy*
II Corinthians 8:12-15 ..... *a question of equality and abundance*
II Corinthians 9:6-15 .... *God loves a cheerful giver*
Galatians 2:10 .... *remember the poor*
James 2:1-9 .... *rich, poor and God's bias*
James 2:14-17,26 .... *faith without works is dead*
I John 3:17-18 .... *loving in deed, not just in word*
I John 4:19-21 .... *cannot love God without loving neighbor*
—Hunger Times

24

Use the Media

By Kimberly Bobo

For better or worse, the media play an increasingly important role in influencing people and in decisions of our elected leaders. Media coverage is, therefore, vital to the work against hunger not as an end in itself but as a means to achieve goals. Good media coverage can give your hunger group and its programs visibility, make community outreach and advocacy easier and enhance the group's credibility. To use the media well, however, we must learn how it works and develop media skills.

Your group's overall goals determine what media to use. For example, to publicize monthly meetings you need to find and learn how to use community calendars. If your goal is more coverage of an issue, develop relationships with news reporters.

Set aside time for your group to discuss how to best focus its media efforts. You must decide upon your target audience, and which media best reaches them. Determine which media are most likely to cover your issues and which reach the most people. Which media coverage will best help meet your goals?

The major media in your community—the large secular newspapers, television and radio stations—reach a large audience but are unlikely to cover small organizations or news they don't consider "hot." Good contacts with individual reporters are important. What reporter has written about hunger in your community? Who covered the African famine? Make getting to know these people a priority even if there is no immediate result.

Small local media are more likely to cover local activities. A weekly community newspaper or a college paper probably will use most news releases that have a local angle. Small radio stations and denominational publications are also likely prospects.

Develop a Media List

First, check the Yellow Pages under radio stations and broadcasting companies, news services, and newspapers. Ask other groups to share their media list with you or help you compile your own. Some advertising companies compile and sell media lists. The reference librarian at your local library can help. Collect the names, addresses and phone numbers of the appropriate people for your media priorities. Before you mail materials, call to check that you have the correct names. The reference materials and your media list will become out-of-date quickly, so update your list regularly. If your group has access to a computer, organize the list on it for easy revision.

News Releases

The most common communication with media is the news release. This is a story or announcement (new) written in a format that is easy for the media to use. Use it to announce special programs or events such as a slide show, the results of a new study on local hunger or the formation of a hunger group or speakers' bureau. News releases can also express shock, concern or support. If the mayor initiates a special program to provide additional food to low-income people, congratulate him or her for compassionate leadership. Such news releases must closely follow events covered by the media. News releases can also announce events or press conferences that you want the media to attend, but do not expect them at every event.

Keep your news release polite, even if you disagree with a vote or position. Address the issues directly; do not question the person's motivations. Conflict may be unavoidable or even instrumental in changing people's positions, but avoid alienating them unnecessarily.

News releases should follow a standard format: typed, doublespaced, on legal or letter size white paper. Leave wide margins on all four sides. Put the first page on letterhead stationery if you have it. In the upper left corner single space the name and phone number(s) of the person to call for further information. If you don't have letterhead paper, type the group's name, address and phone number single-spaced at the top left-hand corner of the first page. On the right side of the page give the date on which you wrote the release. A few spaces below the date, give the time at which your story can be released. Most often, your news release will read "For Immediate Release," but it can give a specific date and time, such as "For Release on July 1, 1987." Place a slug line (a one or two word title) at the left side of the page on line 30. Begin your release below the halfway mark on the first page. If the release is longer than one page, type "more" at the bottom of each page except the last. On the second and following pages type the slug line and the page number. Type "-30-" at the end of the news release: standard notation for the end. Try to keep your news release to two pages or less.

The first paragraph has to be crammed with facts: who, what, where, when and sometimes why. Put the most important information at the beginning of the release since editors tend to cut from the bottom. Write in an objective style. Give short statements of facts with only a few sentences in each paragraph. To get your group's opinion into the release quote someone—yourself, if necessary, or the chair of the board or another member of your group. You may feel silly doing this at first, but it is standard procedure. Information about your group usually goes in the last paragraph and unfortunately is frequently cut. Special documents, letters or statements that reporters need to have in full can be sent as attachments. If you are unsure to whom the news release should be sent, address it to the City Editor at the major daily paper, the Managing Editor at weeklies and the News Director or News Assignment Editor at radio and television stations.

Letter-to-the-Editor

Letters-to-the-editor are the second most widely read feature in most papers and can be a good vehicle for public education and sometimes for advocacy. Any time an article misses a possible hunger angle, recruit someone in your group to write immediately. You must send or hand deliver your letter within a day or two of when the article first appeared. Timeliness is everything to the editor. If you want the letter-to-the-editor to give visibility to your hunger group, ask the person who writes it to give her association with the group—for example, Susie Smith, President, Holy Trinity Episcopal Hunger Committee. Such an identification both offers visibility and shows the writer's authority for writing on the issue.

Newspaper Interviews

An interview with a reporter is easier than you might expect. The hardest part is arranging it. It is best to schedule interviews for others and have others schedule them for you. If possible, identify the appropriate reporter ahead of time. If you're not sure who to talk to, call the newspaper and ask for the city desk, which is responsible for assigning reporters to stories. Give a brief picture of what the interviewee has to say and ask who to talk to. Work to interest the reporter over the phone without giving away the whole story. The key to obtaining an interview is offering interesting, up-to-date information that has local impact. Think through the local angle on your story and mention it briefly.

The person to be interviewed should practice responding to likely questions. Think of some pithy, quotable statements because reporters appreciate lively quotes. Make copies of materials to leave with the reporter. Be prompt and dress appropriately. If the interview is conducted at the press office, a photograph is usually taken.

Be careful what you say in an interview. Anything you say may show up in print, even if you say, "Please don't quote me." It's not a fair request. Just don't say it if you are not willing to see it in print. Be sure to give the group's name, a contact person's name and phone number. If you do not ask to have this information listed, it will not be. If you do ask, about half of the time it will.

At the end of the interview ask if the reporter would like to receive your press releases regularly. That is a good way to build your media list. Reporters almost always say yes and are much more apt to use them after personal contact with the group. Do not ask to see the interview before it is printed. It's not standard practice, and reporters find it insulting.

When the interview is printed, write or call to thank the reporter even if the interview is not perfect. In fact, most interviews contain inaccurate statements or material that you would have stressed differently. Expect the article not to be exactly the way you'd like it. Unless it's really awful, do not correct the errors. Use the thank-you as a way to build a relationship with a reporter and to offer assistance for future hunger related articles.

One hunger group, *Results,* has been extremely successful getting positive editorials written about pending hunger legislation by arranging meetings with an editorial writer. Select an issue that needs an editorial and that is the kind of issue about which the paper writes editorials. Ask for the name of the correct editorial writer. Most legislative issues and local policy matters are appropriate for editorial. Rehearse what to say and how to respond to questions. Research the answers by calling a hunger organization or other sources of information.

Talk about the importance of the issue and give additional background information and sources. Far more often than one might think, this process works! Meeting with an editorial writer can produce an editorial supporting or opposing an issue about which your group is concerned. Such editorials are read by elected leaders and the public at large and consequently can influence general public opinion as well as specific votes and decisions.

Radio and Television

Arranging interviews on radio and television talk shows is similar, except they normally need to be scheduled further in advance unless the issue is particularly timely or controversial. Normally send a letter of inquiry to the program manager. Explain who you would like to have interviewed and the issues of interest. State that you will call the program manager in five to ten days. When you call, be prepared to explain why the person should be interviewed and how the issues concern the viewers. If possible, give examples of presentations the person has done that were well received. No program manager wants to schedule someone who will be an embarrassment.

Once an interview is scheduled, send a confirmation letter and include possible questions the interviewer might ask as well as the group's name and address. The name and address are particularly important for television so the station can prepare a message to be flashed on the screen when you tell people how to get involved. Television stations can also use a few of your slides if there's time, and they generally like adding visual interest to the interview.

Practice answering questions calmly and succinctly. If you have anticipated and practiced answering terrible questions, the real thing is bound to be easier. Summarize your main points in a handful of well-phrased themes that are simple and easy to remember. Repeat these themes during your interview.

Obviously, dress doesn't much matter for a radio interview, though it's better to look professional. It does matter for TV. In general wear a simple, solid-colored suit. Bright colors usually broadcast well; neutral shades do not. Avoid jewelry—especially dangling earrings and large, clunky bracelets. Some makeup, especially powder, is good. Ask the program manager's advice.

Arrive early, especially if the interview is live. You may have to fill out forms and sign releases before being interviewed. During the interview look at the person who is talking with you, rather than at the camera. Avoid talking with your hands. Hold onto a pen with both hands in your lap, if necessary. TV magnifies gestures, and they are distracting.

Send the interviewer and/or the program manager a personal thank-you note afterward. Offer yourself as a resource for future shows on hunger and suggest program topics with broad community appeal.

Many radio and TV stations also air editorials: another potential way to get your views across. If your group disagrees with a radio or television editorial, consider replying to it. Particularly if your group is mentioned by name your reply has a good chance of airing because the Federal Communications Commission requires stations to provide equal time for different viewpoints. Call the station and ask how to get equal time for responding to the editorial. Your response will need to be prepared quickly.

Inviting the Media

When you have a newsworthy event or important news to release, you may want to schedule a news conference. Send everyone on your media list a news release. Call all the reporters the day before the event to remind them, emphasizing how newsworthy the event will be. Set up a media table with packets of fact sheets, news releases and background information. Avoid putting too many items into the packets. Assign one person who will not be speaking at the news conference to greet and assist reporters, getting their names and affiliations for future contacts.

The only way to learn to use the media is to try it. Find a person or two in your group to coordinate media efforts, and be persistent. The immediate fruits of your work are easy to measure whether or not you get coverage. The long-term benefits of increased awareness and influence in hunger issues, although harder to measure, are immensely important to ending hunger.

Appendix A: Printed Resources

The following annotated bibliography has been prepared for people who want to study the problem of hunger in more detail or need additional resources for the work against hunger. All the books listed are readable, provide solid information and are well documented.

The books marked with an asterisk (*) can be ordered from **Alternatives, P.O. Box 429, Ellenwood, GA 30049, (404) 961-0102.** Prices subject to change without notice. Prepayment preferred in U.S. Funds. Please add the following amounts to your order for the cost of shipping and handling: Orders under $2.00, add $1.00; orders $2.00 to $10.00, add $2.00; orders $10.00 to $30.00, add $3.50; orders $30.00 to $50.00, add $6.50; orders $50.00 to $100.00, add 10% of order; foreign orders add $2.00 to above charges.

The Problem of Hunger

Bryon, William, ed. *The Causes of World Hunger.* New York: Paulist Press, 1983. 256 pp. $8.95. A chapter on each major cause of hunger (colonialism, abuse of resources, refugees, excessive arms spending, etc.). Each chapter written by a present or former board member of Bread for the World, the Christian citizens' lobby.

Dorr, Donal. *Spirituality and Justice.* Maryknoll, NY: Orbis Books. 214 pp., 1985, $10.95. Challenges Christians to combine social action and spirituality and to increase their involvement in work for justice.

Fenton, Thomas P. and Heffron, Mary J. *Food, Hunger, Agribusiness: a Directory of Resources.* Maryknoll, NY: Orbis Books, 1987. 132 pp., $9.95. A comprehensive, up-to-date listing of organizations, books, periodicals, pamphlets, audiovisuals and other resources.

Fenton, Thomas P. and Heffron, Mary J. *Third World Resource Directory.* Maryknoll, NY: Orbis Books, 1984, $17.95. Contains the same kinds of material listed above. The same people have also compiled resource directories on Asia and Pacific, Latin America and Caribbean, and Women in the Third World.

Freudenberger, C. Dean. *Food for Tomorrow?* Minneapolis: Augsburg Publishing House, 1984. 174 pp., $9.95. A Christian economist looks at the world crisis in agriculture and calls for a recovery of the biblical basis for care of our environment.

George, Susan. *Ill Fares the Land: Essays on Food, Hunger, and Power.* Washington, DC: Institute for Policy Studies, 1984. 102 pp. $5.95. A collection of essays written between 1979 and 1982 dealing with questions of power and challenging many current assumptions about hunger. Forthright and uncompromising without being strident.

Grant, James P. *The State of the World's Children.* Oxford University Press, 110 pp., $8.95. Compiled annually by the United Nations Children's Fund (UNICEF), the report contains narratives and statistics that paint a country-by-country picture of conditions affecting children, including nutrition, health, education, population and economic performance.

* Hombs, Mary Ellen, and Snyder, Mitch. *Homelessness in America: A Forced March to Nowhere.* Community for Creative Non-Violence, 146 pp., 1982. $5.00. A thorough examination of the situation facing the homeless in the United States, augmented by powerful photography and testimonies offered to Congress by Hombs and Snyder.

Kutzner, Patricia L., and Lagoudakis, Nickola. *Who's Involved with Hunger: An Organizational Guide.* Washington, DC: World Hunger Education Service, 1985. $8. Helpful comments about organizations and agencies working to end hunger.

*Lappé, Frances Moore, and Collins Joseph. *Food First: Beyond the Myth of Scarcity.* New York: Ballantine. Revised 1979, $2.95. Question and answer format; comprehensive study of the economic and political causes of hunger.

Lappé, Francis Moore, and Collins, Joseph. *World Hunger: Twelve Myths.* Grove Press, 208 pp., 1986. $7.95. Essential reading for those who believe every person has a right to life-sustaining resources. Compelling, well-researched answers to the myths and mistaken beliefs every hunger activist encounters.

Nelson, Jack A. *Hunger for Justice: The Politics of Food and Faith.* Maryknoll, NY: Orbis Books. 320 pp., 1980, $7.95. Puts together biblical themes with political and economic analysis to confront the outrage of needless hunger.

*Nelson-Pallmeyer, Jack. *The Politics of Compassion.* Orbis books, 132 pp., 1986, $8.95. Written by a non-poor person for the non-poor with the concern that if we cut ourselves off from the transforming wisdom and insights of the poor "we guarantee our own destruction.".

*Peters, Arno. *World Map: Peters Projection.* Friendship Press, 1979. $7.95. Educational tool designed to correct the colonial bias of traditional maps which exaggerate the size of continents in the northern hemisphere. Presents all countries according to their true surface area.

Toten, Suzanne C. *World Hunger: The Responsibility of Christian Education.* Maryknoll, NY: Orbis Books, 210 pp., 1982, $7.95. Brings together in one volume all the resources on hunger that are useful for an educator. Theory and practice; avoids moralizing but speaks truth to power.

*Sider, Ronald J. *Rich Christians in an Age of Hunger: A Biblical Study.* Downers Grove, IL: InterVarsity Press, 1977. 249 pp., $5.95. Revised and expanded, this edition updates the author's biblical and factual discussion of the responsibility of U.S. Christians in a time of world hunger.

Simon, Arthur, *Bread for the World.* Ramsey, NJ, Paulist Press. 219 pp., revised 1984, $4.95. Classic on hunger and Christian responsibility. Moving and human analysis of the social and economic causes of hunger. An excellent introduction for those new to hunger issues and an up-to-date overview for those long involved.

Sivard, Ruth Leger. *World Military and Social Expenditures.* Leesburg, VA.: WMSE Publications. 46 pp., revised annually, $4.00. Documents proportionate amounts spent on military and on social services such as education and health care.

Effective Organizing

Bobo, Kimberley. *Lives Matter: A Handbook for Christian Organizing.* Kansas City: Sheen & Ward. 200 pp., 1987, $8.95. Kim Bobo draws on more than ten years' experience with Bread for the World in presenting practical approaches and techniques for starting and maintaining a group, public speaking, lobbying elected officials and using the media.

Center for Conflict Resolution. *A Manual for Group Facilitators.* Philadelphia: New Society Press. 88 pp., 1985, $6.00. Working manual for learning to communicate well, plan effectively, solve problems creatively, deal with conflict and move groups toward fulfillment of their own goals. Discusses values, dynamics and common sense behind effective group processes that have been tested and demonstrated.

135

Church World Service/CROP. *Organizational Guide for a CROP Hunger Walk.* Elkhart, IN: Church World Service/CROP. (Order from address on p. 148.) Includes step-by-step timeline, committees needed, publicity guidelines and almost everything else needed to organize a small to medium-sized hunger walk. Field tested in hundreds of communities!

Flanagan, Joan. *Grassroots Fundraising.* 1981, $12.00.

Fleming, Peter. *Church and Press: Friend or Foe? How to Be Friends.* New York: the United Church of Christ Office of Communication, 8 pp., 1982. This handy booklet helps local congregations develop good media relations.

Food Research and Action Center. *How to Document Hunger in Your Community.* Washington, DC: Food Research and Action Center, 1983. By researching such areas as changes in health, demand, and economic data, you can find out about hunger in your own neighborhood.

Kahn, Si. *Organizing: A Guide for Grassroots Leaders.* New York: McGraw-Hill Book Company. 1981, $7.95.

*Longacre, Paul. *Fund Raising Projects with a World Hunger Emphasis.* Herald Press, 70 pp., 1980. $1.95. Twenty-one ideas for families and church groups wanting to raise money and increase their understanding of hunger at the same time.

Rossie, Chuck, Ed. *Media Resource guide.* Los Angeles: Foundation for American Communications, 48pp.,1985. Practical guide explaining how your group can get the attention of newspaper and how to present information in interesting and usable ways.

Direct Assistance

Arnold, John. *Give Me Your Hungry: Food Pantry Operational Handbook.* St. Louis: Salvation Army. A how-to for large-scale food pantries. Full of practical details based on years of experience.

Beckman, David M. and Donnelly, Elizabeth Anne. *The Overseas List.* Minneapolis: Augsburg Publishing House. 192 pp., 1979. Comprehensive listing of development-related opportunities for voluntary service and employment abroad.

Bread for the World. *Hunger Watch U.S.A.* Washington, DC: Bread for the World, 1985. This manual includes questionnaires about the operation and effectiveness of U.S. food assistance programs, to allow you to document hunger in your community.

Buell, Becky. *Alternatives to the Peace Corps: Gaining Third World Experience.* San Francisco: Food First. 36 pp., 1987, $3. Raises questions about the role of volunteers in third world countries and gives suggestions on the best volunteer programs.

Food First.*Education for Action: Graduate Studies with a Focus on Social Change.* San Francisco: Food First. 55 pp., 1987, $3.00. Listing of progressive programs in agriculture, anthropology, development, international studies, economics, nutrition, and many more.

Maryland Food Committee. *Plain Talk About Emergency Food Centers.* Baltimore: Maryland Food Committee. A food center how-to.

Wright-Deitelbaum, Dianne. *How to Start a Food Pantry.* Los Angeles: Interfaith Hunger Coalition. 17 pp., 1984. Written for groups setting up pantries in Los Angeles, but useful anywhere. Write Interfaith Hunger Coalition, 1010 South Flower Street, Suite 404, Los Angeles, CA 90015.

Advocacy

Bread for the World: 820 Rhode Island Ave. NE, Washington, DC 20018. They have an extensive catalog of background papers, organizing kits, voting records, bulletin inserts and other resources related to lobbying and to current national legislation about hunger. Write for a complete catalog.

Friends Committee on National Legislation: "How-to Series." 245 Second Street, NE, Washington, DC 20002. Seven pamphlets on various aspects of lobbying.

League of Women Voters.

Getting Out the Vote: a Guide for Running Registration and Voting Drives. 1984, 16 pp., $1.25. Practical information on organizing a drive, working with volunteers and election officials and maintaining nonpartisanship.

Making an Issue of It: The Campaign Handbook. 1976, 12 pp., $1.50. A lobbying how-to.

Tell It to Washington. Updated every two years. $1.00. Lists House and Senate members and major committee assignments. Includes Supreme Court justices, cabinet officers and useful Washington phone numbers. Tips on effective lobbying.

All available from the League of Women Voters, 1730 M Street NW, Washington, DC 20036.

*Simon, Arthur. *Christian Faith and Public Policy: No Grounds for Divorce* Grand Rapids, MI. Eerdman's William B., Pub. Co. 1987. 120 pp., $6.95. Points out the inseparability of Christian faith and social concern.

Responsible Living

*Alternatives, ed. *To Celebrate: Reshaping Holidays and Rites of Passage.* Ellenwood, GA: Alternatives. 224 pp., 1987, $10.00. For those not satisfied with the models of celebration offered by a consumer society. Celebrations that nourish human relationships and celebrate the human spirit. Resources for alternative celebrations of all major holidays and rites of passage in our culture, including resources for personal meditation and corporate worship.

*Bodner, Joan, ed. *Taking Charge of Our Lives, Living Responsibly in the World.* American Friends Service Committee, Harper and Row, 254 pp., 1984. $8.95. A classic on responsible living. Revised edition surveys areas of life where people are most captivated by consumerism and most eager to change. Provides values clarification exercises to help readers examine use of time, food, shelter, community, aging, work, children, health care and energy. Practical suggestions for change.

Domini, Amy. *Ethical Investing.* Reading, MA: Addison-Wesley. 256 pp., 1984, $17.95. Stockbroker offers a good primer for those wanting to know more about investments consistent with their values. Useful to the novice or experienced investor.

Foster, Richard J. *Freedom of Simplicity.* San Francisco: Harper & Row. 192pp., 1981. $11.50. Challenging yet comforting book sets the quest for simple living in the context of holistic Christian maturity. Explores the complicated decisions and discipline involved in living a faithful life in today's world.

The Funding Exchange. *Directory of Socially Responsible Investments.* The Funding Exchange, 135 East 15th St., New York, NY 10003. $5.00. Useful guide to a wide range of mutual and money market funds, investment advisors and organizations. Includes a section on groups specializing in funding low-income community projects. Good bibliography of publications about ethical investing.

* Gish, Arthur. *Beyond the Rat Race.* Herald Press, 192 pp., 1981. $6.95. Practical and philosophical insight into most areas of life. Clear, forthright and compelling presentation. Originally published in 1973, this classic on responsible living has been revised and enlarged.

* Lappé, Francis Moore and Family. *What to Do After You Turn Off the TV: Fresh Ideas for Enjoying Family Time.* Ballantine Books, 197 pp., 1985. $7.95. To order: Send $9.00 to INA Books, 5934 Ayala, Oakland, CA 94609. Alternatives for those who watch too much TV, from arts and crafts to cooking and baking, from educational experiences to just plain fun.

*Longacre, Doris Janzen. *Living More with Less.* Herald Press 294 pp., 1980. $8.95. Practical suggestions on clothing, housing, transportation, recreation and more. Combines theory and practice.

* Longacre, Doris Janzen. *More-with-Less Cookbook.* Herald Press, 328 pp., 1976. $11.95. Designed to "prod over-fed North Americans to do something about our overabundance in relation to the world food crisis, this comprehensive cookbook is full of ideas for better, more responsible eating through low-cost, low-fat, low-sugar and less protein—inexpensive recipes.

* O'Grady, Ron. *Tourism in the Third World, Christian Reflections.* Orbis Books, 81 pp., 1981. $6.95. Alternatives for learning about other cultures through non-exploitative travel and a call for the church to get involved in tourism education, helping build friendships and transform lives.

* Voran, Marilyn Helmuth. *Add Justice to Your Shopping List.* Herald Press, 69 pp., 1986. $3.95. Guide for reshaping food buying habits. Promotes economy, nutrition and justice as basic ingredients for menu planning. Invites readers to look at how grocery shopping in the U.S. is connected to world hunger.

Winn, Grace, ed. *Simply Delicious: Quantity Cooking for churches.* Ellenwood, GA: Alternatives. 100 pp., 1983, $4.50. Active Presbyterian laywoman gives guidelines, suggestions, recipes and menus for cooking responsibly for large groups.

Working in a Local Congregation

Bread for the World has a number of resources for congregational study, worship and action planning. Among them:

"All God's Children." A dialogue designed to be read by children, it compares the lives of young people in rich and poor countries.

"Behold, I Am Making All Things New." Two persons dialogue addresses the relationship between personal religion and social activism. Good for small group discussions or as a dialogue sermon in a worship service.

Voices from the Quiet. A chancel drama appropriate for worship services. Addresses the problems of taking hunger seriously and getting involved. Complete catalog available from Bread for the World at the address on page 148.

Brown, Robert McAfee. *Unexpected News: Reading the Bible with Third World Eyes.* Philadelphia: Westminster Press. 166 pp., 1984, $7.95. A North American theologian introduces and interprets contemporary Latin American Christianity.

Church World Service/Crop. *Educational Resources.* Elkhart, IN: Church World Service. A booklet designed for hunger walk recruiters to help promote understanding, enable reflection and encourage action.

Pierce, Gregory F. *Activism That Makes Sense: Congregation and Community Organization.* Ramsey, NJ: Paulist Press. 1984, $6.95 Why and how community involvement fosters self-interest.

Lutheran Hunger Program (Complete catalogue available from the address on

p. 145.)

"Zacchaeus and the 'reedom Fund," by David Tiede. 4-page Bible study on Luke 19:1-10. Single copy free.

"These on Land in the Bible," by Walter Brueggemann. 4 pages. Single copy free.

"The Biblical Roots of Justice," by Jose Miguez Bonino. 12 pages, along with other papers presented at conferences in 1982 and 1987. $2.

"Rich Man and Poor Lazarus," by George S. Johnson. Adult Bible study on Luke 16:19-31. Single copy free.

"Why People are Poor," by Tom Hanks. 4-page survey of oppression in the Bible. Single copy free.

"God's Food: the Relation Between Holy Communion and World Hunger," by Gail Ramshaw-Schmidt. 31 page booklet.

Hanks, Thomas D. *God So Loved The Third World: The Bible, the Reformation and Liberation Theologies.* Orbis, New York. 176 pp., 198, $8.95.

*New Jewish Agenda. *The Shalom Seders, Three Passover Haggadahs.* Adama Books, 101 pp., 1984. $12.95. Freedom is the predominant theme at Passover, and these three Haggadahs explore the experience of bondage, exodus and liberation through a contemporary lens. Uses traditional Seder elements in shaping an experience that will be meaningful to both Jews and non-Jews. Can be used within family or in a larger group setting.

Seeds. *Roots of Hope.* Decatur, GA, Seeds, 80 pp. 1979. $1.95. 52 miss-a-meal meditations by staff and friends of Seeds Magazine.

*Sider, Ronald J., Ed. *Cry Justice: The Bible speaks on Hunger and Poverty.* Ramsey, NJ: Paulist Press, 1980. 220 pp., $3.95. A handy collection of almost everything the Bible says about poverty, hunger and justice. Helpful study questions included.

Curricula for Adults

Bread for the World Educational Fund. *Hunger in a Land of Plenty.* Seven study sessions on domestic hunger with topics ranging from discovering who is poor and hungry and why to developing actions to take in a local community.

A Hungry World. This basic study of world hunger covers facts and attitudes about hunger, its causes and solutions, biblical perspectives and action suggestions. a leader's guide is contained in the volume, with suggestions for group participation.

Land and Hunger: A Biblical Worldview. Study course which explores patterns of land ownership and land reform. Includes background reading, discussion, activities, biblical reflection and simulation exercises.

All available from Bread for the World at the Address on page 148.

The Christian Life Commission of the Southern Baptist Convention.

"The Bible Speaks on Hunger." $.15 each.

"Old Testament Bible Studies for a World Hunger Emphasis"

"New Testament Bible Studies for a World Hunger Emphasis"

$1 for five of either title. (Order from the address on p. 147.)

Church World Service Office on Global Education. *Scriptural Poster-Related Curricula.* Baltimore: Church World Service Office on Global Education, 1984. Each poster is on a specific hunger topic. Posters available for $3 as a set of six only. Curriculum guides on each topic available separately for $.50 each. Order from Church World Service: address on page 148.

Dodd, Dee Anne, ed. *Hunger and Militarism: A Guide to Study, Reflection and*

Action. New York: American Friends Service Committee, 1984.

Fitzpatrick, James and Karen, with James and Kathleen McGinnis. *Those Who Hunger*. Ramsey, NJ: Paulist Press, 1984. $2.50. Designed as a Lenten resource, this seven-session study course will involve participants in an exploration of hunger that goes deeper than just facts, figures and analyses. The kit includes tabloids for participants, guides for leaders, and a slide/tape presentation.

*Garcia, Ana de and Johnson, George S. *Evangelism and the Poor*. Augsburg Press, 39 pp., 1986. $1.50. Calls the church to combine evangelistic efforts with enlightened compassion for the needs of the poor. Five study sessions. Easy-to-read format with class assignments ranging from Bible study to hands-on work with the poor.

Jorgenson, Bonnie, and Simon, Arthur. *Too Many Are Hungry: What Can I Do?* Kansas City: Leaven Press, 1985. Study sessions examining world hunger from a Biblical perspective.

*Friesen, Delores Histand. *Living More with Less Study/Action Guide*. Herald Press, 111 pp., 1981. $5.95. Designed to accompany Doris Janzen Longacre's *Living More with Less*. Good study guide for church schools or others exploring lifestyle changes.

Curricula for Intergenerational Use

Adams-Williams, Jan, McMillan, Judy and Thornberry, Milo. *Those Who Speak for God: Household Studies on the Minor Prophets*. Ellenwood, GA: Alternatives. 28 pp., 1984, $1.50. The Old Testament "Minor Prophets" whose searing words about integrity between faith professed and faith lived are as timely— and irritating—in the 20th century as they were in ancient Israel. A nine session intergenerational resource.

*Dregni, Meredith S. *Experiencing More with Less: An Intergenerational Curriculum for Camps, Retreat and Other Educational Settings*. Scottsdale, PA: Herald Press, 104 pp., 1983. $4.95. Designed for families and groups of all ages who come together to explore the theme of living more simply, responsibly and lovingly. Curriculum guide for five days of program, based on the book *Living More with Less* by Doris Janzen Longacre.

Feed the World: A Crisis Curriculum. Prepared by Coalition for Alternatives in Jewish Education. 48 pp., 1986. Contains background on hunger issues and Jewish teachings, with strategies and suggestions for Jewish holiday observances, prayers, Bible studies, and action and fundraising ideas.

Curricula for Youth and Children

The Board for Social Ministry Services The Lutheran Church-Missouri Synod. *A Festival of Sharing*. A hunger program weekend for youths. Order from address on page 145.

Bread for The World. *Bread for the World on Campus: A Resource Kit*. Washington, DC: Bread for the World, 1983. This kit enables students, faculty and campus ministers to integrate public policy information and action into campus life.

Ciekot, Jerold, and Douglas Gwyn. *Ending Hunger: It's Possible, It's Happening*. American Friends Service Committee, New York, 1979. $5.50. Packet contains simulation game, action project suggestions, background readings. Six week study format, suitable for teens and adults. (Order from American Friends Service Committee at the address on page 146.)

Foote, Sharon. Resource packets for children:

Plant a Seed, for 3, 4 and 5 year olds
Begin to Care, Begin to Share, for younger elementary children
Learning to Care, Learning to Share , for older elementary children.
Nashville: Discipleship Resources, revised 1983. $5 each. Each packet contains a curriculum and assortment of supporting resources. Draws heavily on material from the Heifer Project which provides livestock and training in third world countries. Designed for Vacation Bible School but adaptable to other formats.

Hendrix, Lela M. *Hunger Alert: An Awareness/Action Guide for Youth and Youth Leaders*. Nashville: Christian Life Commission of the Southern Baptist Convention. Packet, 1984, $3.00. Comprehensive plans for an emphasis on world and domestic hunger for youth and youth leader. Bible study, worship suggestions, hymn, skit, case study, field trip, food and fundraising suggestions. (Order from address on p. 147.)

Impact on Hunger.
World Hunger: Learning to Meet the Challenge. Public school curriculum for high school students.
Hunger and the Catholic Tradition Companion book providing supplementary religious instruction.
New York: Impact on Hunger, 1985. (Order from Impact at the address on p. 149.)

Lersch, Phil and Jean, and Munson, Bonnie. *Homelessness: Activities About People Who Are Homeless*. St. Petersburg, FL: Brethren House Ministries. 1987. Student book: 20 pp., $2.75 (discount for bulk copies). Teacher book: 8 pp., $1.00. For junior high students. Designed for use in Christian schools or churches. Can be modified for use in public schools. Background information; 14 suggested activities to help students gather new facts; questionnaires to use before and after to measure learning. (Order from address on p. 148.).

Oxfam America. *Fast for a World Harvest Organizer's Guide*. Boston: Oxfam America. Guide for planned fasts and other activities on college campuses.

*Rifas, Leonard. *Food First Comic*. 24 pp., Food First/IFDP, 1982. $1. Sifts through confusing and often contradictory myths about hunger. An excellent way for junior and senior high school students to begin to understand why people in the world are starving when plenty of food is produced.

*Rubin, Laurie. *Food First Curriculum: An Integrated Curriculum for Grade 6*. 146 pp., Food First/IFDP, 1984. $12. Comes with modifications for grades 4-5 and 7-8. Multidisciplinary curriculum designed to help children understand where their food comes from how it gets to them and who gets by-passed in the process.

Scriptographic Books, a division of Channing L. Bete Co. Inc., produces a number of simple, comic-book style booklets, designed to be bought in bulk and used by churches and other organizations. Write them for a catalogue and price list at 200 State Road, South Deerfield, MA 01373. Hunger-related titles include:
"Let's Learn about World Hunger: an Information and Activities Book." 16 pp. For children ages 9-12. Helps children understand hunger and accept responsibility to help abolish it.
"About World Hunger." 8 pp. A coloring and activities book for young children.
"About World Hunger." 16 pp. Summary of hunger issues and the call of the church to be involved. For older children through adult.

Shirman, David. *World Food Day Curriculum*. Baltimore: Church World Service. 24 pp., 1986. For grades 8-12. Lesson plan, teacher resource section and extensive bibliography.

Sprinkle, Patricia H. and Peterson, Tom. *All Tied Up!* Ellenwood, GA: Seeds/ Alternatives. Packet, 1984, $15. Provides everything needed for a youth "lock-in," including publicity posters, menus, songs and suggestions on organizing committees to conduct the event.

World Hunger Year. *A Guide for Action on Food and Hunger in the School and Community.* World Hunger Year (See address on p. 151.) 1979. $5. Lesson plans; resource lists; teacher and student guides. Special emphasis on learning about local problems.

Games and Simulation Exercises

American Friends Service Committee. *Hunger on Spaceship Earth.* New York: American Friends Service Committee. $1.50. Best played with at least 30 people at a meal setting. A how-to manual on hunger meals (See chapter 19.). Includes menu and place setting suggestions for people designated as first, second or third world. (Order from address on p. 146.).

American Friends Service Committee. *The Twenty-first Year: a Simulation Game on Issues in Global Development.* American Friends Service Committee. Comes as part of kit, *Ending Hunger: It's Possible, It's Happening.* 1979, $5.50. Suitable for college age and above. Any number can play. Takes 60 minutes. (Order from American Friends Service Committee at the address on p. 146).

Center for World Development. *Living with the Land: Continuity and Change in a Developing Country.* Denver: Social Studies Schools Services. Kit, 1979. Includes 355 black and white study prints, two guide books with maps and background materials on Ghana. Good material for a case study.

Chapman;, Dr. G.P. and Dowler, Elizabeth. *The Green Revolution Game.* London: Marginal Context Limited, c/o Department of Human Nutrition, London School of Hygiene and Tropical Medicine, Keppel St. (Gower St) London WC1E 7HT United Kingdom. $350. Game set includes a comprehensive game managers' handbook, player handbooks and record sheets, card packs for environment conditions, hazards and births, tokens for equipment and supplies, paper money and an optional computer program. Originally designed as a teaching tool, this elaborate and highly realistic scenario game has been used by development agencies in more than 25 countries. Can be played by between 12 and 24 people and takes four to six hours to complete.

ISU Extension Service. *World Resource Kit.* Collection of resources and activities for junior and senior high school. Available from ISU Extension Service, Box 1427, Cedar Rapids, Iowa 52406.

J. Games Company. Who Needs Enemies. Barnstable, MA: J. Games Company, 1982. For high school students. Simulation game on global issues where teams represent the developed and developing countries and try to end hunger by the year 2000.

*Kishpaugh, Charles R. and Pauline E. *Hungry Decisions: Making Life and Death Choices in Africa, Asia or Latin America.* Nashville: Discipleship Resources, 35 pp., 1982. $2.50. Highly informative and sensitive workbook inviting participants to identify with a third world woman or man trapped by poverty and injustice. The authors provide 16 possible endings to each person's life that are influenced by decisions made by the reader.

Longman. *Rice Farming.* Computer simulation on Apple diskette with teacher's guide and student handouts. Students face problems of rice farmers in India, including drought, insects, marketing difficulties. (Available from Social Studies Schools Services at the address on p. 145.) Lutheran Hunger Program.

*A Road to a Well Fed Village. ALC Hunger Program, 1986. $2. Designed for high school youth; requires 1-3 hours playing time. Challenges players to create a well-fed village—that is, a world with equal distribution of wealth and resources among countries and peoples. Explores responses to the hunger crisis in the context of Christian stewardship.

Population Reference Bureau. Food for Thought. Population Reference Bureau, 1337 Connecticut Ave. NW, Washington, DC 20036. $3. For 25 to 200 people ages 12 and over. Contains instructions and resource materials. Helps players understand the size and growth rate of populations, distribution of population, and distribution and consumption of world food supplies.

*Sprinkle, Patricia H. Hunger: Understanding the Crisis through Games, Dramas and Songs. Atlanta: John Knox Press, 142 pp., 1980. $5.95. The games, skits, songs and other resources in this book help all age groups comprehend world hunger.

St. Louis United Nations Association. Global Kaleidoscope: Simulation Exercise for the Classroom. St. Louis U.N. Association, 7359 Forsyth, St. Louis, MO 63105. Eleven games to help students gain a global perspective on current problems. Age range suggestions for each activity.

Van Beilen, Aileen. Hunger Awareness Dinners: A Planning Manual. Scottsdale, PA: Herald Press, 48 pp., 1978. $.95. Extensive suggestions for the "ultimate" hunger meal, with people divided into 5 different population groups. Suggested recipes, table set-up, programs for before or after the dinner and back-up information.

Western Behavioral Sciences Institute. Star Power. Western Behavioral Sciences Institute, 1150 Silverado, La Jolla, CA 92037. $30. Best used with 25-30 people; can be done with as few as 12. People are divided into three groups, with the wealthiest group having the power to make rules for the game. Resulting frustrations and conflicts are analyzed and discussed after the game is halted.

Appendix B: Audiovisual Aids

The organizations listed below provide audiovisual aids dealing with hunger and development issues. Write or call for their listings which include descriptions and rental fees. Most denominational hunger programs (Appendix C) and national hunger organizations (Appendix D) also have audiovisual aids for rent or free distribution.

American Friends Service Committee
1501 Cherry Street
Philadelphia, PA 19102
(215) 241-7000

Church World Service/CROP
P.O. Box 968
Elkhart, IN 46515
(219) 264-3102

EcuFilm
810 12th Avenue South
Nashville, TN 37203
(800) 251-4091, in Tennessee call
    collect (615) 242-6277

Franciscan Communications
1229 South Santee Street
Los Angeles, CA 90015
(800) 421-8510

Maryknoll Film Library
Maryknoll, NY 10545
(914) 941-7590

Mass Media Ministries
2116 N. Charles Street
Baltimore, MD 21218
(301) 727-3270

Mennonite Central Committee
Resource Library
21 S. 12th Street, Box M
Akron, PA 17501
(717) 859-1151

U.S. Committee for UNICEF
331 East 38th Street
New York, NY 10016
(212) 686-5522

Appendix C:
Denominational Hunger Programs and Agencies

African Methodist Episcopal
Church
Missions Department
African Methodist Episcopal Church,
  Room 1926
475 Riverside Drive
New York, NY 10015
(212) 870-2258

Women's Missionary Society
2311 M Street, N.W.
Washington, D.C. 20037
(202) 337-1335

African Methodist Episcopal Zion
Church
Department of Home Missions,
  Pensions and Relief
P.O. Box 30846
Charlotte, NC 28230
(704) 333-3779

Department of Overseas Missions
African Methodist Episcipal Zion
  Church
Suite 1910
475 Riverside Drive
New York, NY 10115
(212) 870-2952

American Baptist Churches in the
U.S.A.
Hunger Office
American Baptist Churches in the
  U.S.A.
P.O. Box 851
Valley Forge, PA 19482-0851
(215) 768-2204

Assemblies of God
Division of Foreign Missions
Assemblies of God International
  Headquarters
1445 Boonville Avenue
Springfield, MO 65802
(417) 862-2781

Christian Church (Disciples of
Christ)
Division of Homeland Ministries
222 S. Downey Avenue
P.O. Box 1986
Indianapolis, In 46206
(317) 353-1491

Christian Methodist Episcopal
Church
General Board of Social Concerns
P.O. Box 92284
Atlanta, GA 30314
(404) 525-8827

Christian Reformed Church in
North America
Christian Reformed World Relief
  Committee
2850 Kalamazoo Avenue, SE
Grand Rapids, MI 49560
(616) 246-0740

Church of God (Anderson, IN)
Board of Church Extension and Home
  Missions
Box 2069
Anderson, IN 46018
(317) 644-2555

Church of God (Cleveland, TN)
World Missions
Keith Street at 25th NW
Cleveland, TN 37311
(615) 472-3361

Church of the Brethren
Brethren House Ministries
6301 56th Ave., N.
St. Petersburg, FL 33709
(813)544-2911

Global Justice
Church of the Brethren—Washington
Office
110 Maryland Avenue, N.E.
Box 50
Washington, D.C. 20002
(202) 546-3202

World Ministries Commission
1451 Dundee Avenue
Elgin, IL 60120
(312) 742-5100

Church of the Nazarene
Division of World Mission
6401 The Paseo
Kansas City, MO 64131
(816) 333-7000

**National Council of the Churches
of Christ in the U.S.A.**
Ecumenical Domestic Hunger Network
Division of Church and Society
475 Riverside Drive, Rm. 572
New York, NY 10115
(212)870-2307

The Episcopal Church
Episcopal Hunger Office
815 Second Avenue
New York, NY 10017
(212) 867-8400

*Presiding Bishop's fund for World
Relief*
(same address as above)

The Evangelical Covenant Church
Covenant World Relief
5101 N. Francisco Avenue
Chicago, IL 60625
(312) 784-3000

**The Evangelical Lutheran Church
in America**
Lutheran Hunger Program
8765 West Higgins Rd.
Chicago, IL 60631
(312)380-2700

Jewish Organizations
*Coalition for Advancement of Jewish
Education*
468 Park Avenue South, Room 904
New York, NY 10016
(212)696-0740

*American Jewish Joint Distribution
Committee*
711 3rd Ave.
New York NY 10017
(212) 687-6200

Mazon
2940 Westwood Blvd. #7
Los Angeles, CA 90064
(213) 470-7769

New Jewish Agenda
64 Fulton St., Ste. 1100
New York, NY 10038
(212) 227-5885

**The Lutheran Church-Missouri
Synod**
World Hunger Concerns Contact:
Dr. Melvin E. Witt
*Department of Stewardship and
Financial Support*
International Center
1333 South Kirkwood Road
Saint Louis, MO 63122-7295
(314) 965-9000

Domestic Hunger Concerns Contact:
Dr. Al Senske
*Board for Social Ministries Services
and World Relief*
1333 South Kirkwood Road
Saint Louis, MO 63122-7912

Mennonite Church
Mennonite Central Committee
21 South 12th Street
Akron, PA 17501
(717) 859-1151

Moravian Church in America
Moravian Church in America
Board of Christian Education
Drawer Y, Salem Station
Winston-Salem, NC 27108
(919) 722-8126

*Department of Education Ministries
and Board of World Mission*
P.O. Box 1245
1021 Center Street
Bethlehem, PA 18016
(215) 867-7566

**National Baptist Convention,
U.S.A., Inc.**
Foreign Mission Board
P.O. Box 3873
Station D
Philadelphia, PA 19146
(215) 735-7868

The Presbyterian Church (U.S.A.)
Before fall, 1988:
The Presbyterian Hunger Program
341 Ponce de Leon Ave., NE
Atlanta, GA 30365
(404)873-1531
or

*475 Riverside Drive, Room 1268
New York, NY 10115
(212)870-3107 or 3108*

After September, 1988:
*The Presbyterian Hunger Program
100 Witherspoon
Louisville, KY 40202-1396*

**Progressive National Baptist
Convention, Inc.**
Home Mission Board
601 50th Street, NE
Washington, D.C. 20019
(202) 396-0558

Reformed Church in America
Program and World Mission
Reformed Church in America
475 Riverside Drive, 18th Floor
New York, NY 10115
(212) 870-3071

**Religious Society of Friends
(Quakers)**
American Friends Service Committee
1501 Cherry Street
Philadelphia, PA 19102
(215) 241-7000

*Friends Committee on National
Legislation*
245 Second Street, NE
Washington, D.C. 20002
(202) 547-6000

**Reorganized Church of Jesus
Christ of Latter Day Saints**
The Hunger Committee
P.O. Box 1059
Independence, MO 64051

The Roman Catholic Church
Campaign for Human Development
U.S. Catholic Conference
1312 Massachusetts Avenue, NW
Washington, D.C. 20005
(202) 659-6650

Catholic Charities, U.S.A.
1319 F Street, N.W., 4th floor
Washington, D.C. 20004
(202) 639-8400

Catholic Relief Services
1011 First Avenue
New York, NY 10022
(212) 838-4700

Conference of Major Superiors of Men
8808 Cameron Street
Silver Spring, MD 20910
(301) 588-4030

*Leadership Conference of Women
Religious*
8808 Cameron Street
Silver Spring, MD 20910
(301) 588-4955

*Office of International Justice and
Peace*
U.S. Catholic Conference
(address above)
(202)659-6812

Southern Baptist Convention
Christian Life Commission
901 Commerce, #550
Nashville, TN 37203
(615)244-2495

Human Needs Department
Foreign Mission Board
P.O. Box 6597
Richmond, Va 23230
(804)353-1051

Home Mission Board
1350 Spring Street, NW
Atlanta, GA 30367-5601
(404) 873-4041

Woman's Missionary Union
100 Missionary Ridge
Highway 280-E
Birmingham, AL 35243
(205) 991-8100

Unitarian Universalist Association
*Unitarian Universalist Service
    Committee, Inc.*
78 Beacon Street
Boston, MA 02108
(617) 742-2120

United Church of Christ
Hunger Action Office
United Church of Christ
475 Riverside Drive, 16th floor
New York, NY 10115
(212) 870-2951

The United Methodist Church
Board of Church and Society
100 Maryland Avenue, NE
Washington, D.C. 20002
(202) 488-5600

Board of Discipleship
P.O. Box 840
Nashville, TN 37202
(615) 327-2700

Board of Global Ministries
475 Riverside Drive
New York, NY 10115
(212) 870-3600

Appendix D: Some Key Organizations

The following organizations are only a small fraction of those doing hunger-related work. We have used two criteria in selecting this list: organizations that can provide assistance and/or resources to assist you in doing the kinds of work outlined in this book, and organizations that are named in one or more chapters. The fact that an organization is not listed does not imply that they are not doing good work.

Alternatives, Box 429, Ellenwood, GA 30049, (404) 961-4622
Provides information and resources to encourage more responsible celebrations and more conscientious ways of living. Sales of books and materials help support non-profit activities such as the campaign to decommercialize Christmas and Easter. Craft shop carries high-quality handmade goods from self-help craft cooperatives in the United States and the third world.

American Community Gardening Association, P.O. Box 400, Glencoe, IL 60022, (312) 835-0250
Nonprofit organization of professional garden organizers, supporters and neighborhood leaders committed to improving communities through horticulture. Publishes quarterly *Journal of Community Gardening.*

Bread for the World, 802 Rhode Island Avenue, N.E., Washington, DC 20018, (202) 269-0200

A Christian citizen's movement that focuses solely on hunger issues. Members organized by congressional district lobby representatives to obtain government policies that address the basic causes of hunger. Publishes "Leaven," a quarterly newsletter. Extensive catalog of background materials, study guides, and worship aids for congregations.

Brethren House Ministries, 6301 56th Avenue, N., St. Petersburg, FL 33709

Gears educational resources on hunger, poverty, and justice to young people.

Children's Defense Fund (CDF), 122 C Street, N.W., Washington, DC 20001, (202) 628-8787

Provides long range and systematic advocacy on behalf of the nation's children. Seeks to change policies and practices which result in the neglect of children.

Church World Service/CROP, *Office on Global Education,* 2115 N. Charles Street, Baltimore, MD 21218, (301) 727-6106

In addition to responding to emergency disasters overseas, supports existing initiatives in global education in the United States. Provides many educational resources, especially for use by church groups.

CROP(Community Hunger Appeal of Church World Service), P.O. Box 968, Elkhart, IN 46515, (219) 264-3102

Organizes more than 2000 CROP Walks to raise money for hunger relief and development efforts of member denominations. Provides organizing materials and guidelines for CROP Walk organizers as well as extensive print and audiovisual resources.

Center for Global Education, Augsburg College, 731-21st Avenue South, Minneapolis, MN 55454, (612)330-1159

Sets up study trips to third world countries, particularly in Latin America. Monthly newsletter, *Global Perspectives*, and periodic regional and national gatherings of study tour participants provide a support network and continuing information.

Community Nutrition Institute (CNI), 2001 S. Street, Suite 530, N.W., Washington, DC 20009, (202) 462-4700

Specializes in food and nutrition issues. Trains anti-hunger groups, represents consumer interests on issues such as nutrition labeling, publishes weekly newsletter "Nutrition Week." Information on federal food programs available.

Co-op America, 2100 M St. NW, Suite 310, Washington, DC 20063, (202) 872-5307

Promotes and networks among cooperatives in the United States. Publishes quarterly magazine, *Building Economic Alternatives.*

Council on Economic Priorities, 30 Irving Place, New York, NY 10003, (212) 420-1133

Monthly newsletter to members on issues of corporate responsibility, defense policy and the environment. Also publishes three to six book-length studies per year.

Friends of the Third World, Inc., 611 West Wayne St., Fort Wayne, IN 46802, (219)422-6821

Alternative trading organization provides educational materials and activities and promotes voluntary action on problems of poverty. Helped form the U.S. Union of Third World Shoppes, a coalition of non-profit groups selling handcrafts made by low income people in the third world and the United

States. Provides information on crafts producers and networking and publicity for alternative trading.

Fund for an Open Society, 311 S. Juniper, Suite 400, Philadelphia, PA 19107, (215) 735-6915.
Non-profit mortgage company provides investment opportunities for socially-minded individuals and organizations to fund mortgages for whites and minorities in racially diverse neighborhoods.

Food Research and Action Center (FRAC), 1319 F Street, N.W., Washington, DC 20004, (202) 393-5060
Nonprofit law firm and advocacy center working with the poor to alleviate hunger in the United States. Works primarily with federal food programs, not only to meet immediate needs but also as an organizing tool for poor people and their allies in the larger effort to create meaningful social change. Provides written materials, training and organizing help for local groups.

Impact on Hunger, 145 E. 49th Street, 3rd floor, New York, NY 10017, (212) 750-9893
Designs hunger curricula for high schools and works to influence educational institutions.

Interfaith Center for Corporate Responsibility, 475 Riverside Drive, Rm. 566, New York, NY 10115, (212) 870-2295
Publishes monthly newsletter *The Corporate Examiner.* ICCR's Clearinghouse on Alternative Investments produces a variety of publications and provides services on alternative investments for 235 member churches and other groups.

Institute for Food and Development Policy, 145 Ninth St., San Francisco, CA 94103, (415) 864-8555
Research, documentation and education center focusing on food and agriculture. Investigates root causes of hunger, including policies of governments and corporations. Also examines and reports how people around the world work for food security and what can be learned from their difficulties and successes.

Interfaith Action for Economic Justice, 110 Maryland Avenue, Suite 509, N.E., Washington, DC 20002, (202) 543-2800
Organized as a cooperative effort of two dozen religious agencies, seeks to shape U.S. policy so as to achieve a greater measure of justice for the needy. Provides detailed background on legislative issues.

National Charities Information Bureau, 19 Union Square West, 6th Floor, New York, NY 10003-3395, (212)929-6300
Independent monitoring of philanthropies. Publishes bimonthly list called "Wise Giving Guide" and individual reports on the organizations listed.

National Committee for World Food Day, 1001 22nd Street, N.W., Washington, DC 20437, (202) 653-2404
Provides information about World food Day activities across the country. Mailings also feature resources available on legislative issues.

National Federation of Community Development Credit Unions, 577 Sixth Street, Brooklyn, NY 11215, (212)768-7859
Member-governed coalition of credit unions which serve low-income communities. Provides training, technical assistance and advocacy services for member credit unions.

National IMPACT Network, 100 Maryland Avenue, Suite 502, N.E., Washington, DC 20002, (202) 544-8636
An interfaith organization which lobbies both national and state legislatures on

social justice issues. Annual workshop trains organizers for effective advocacy.

National Student Campaign Against Hunger, 29 Temple Place, Boston, MA 02111, (617)292-4823

Network of student hunger activists organized through Public Interest Research Groups (PIRGS) in 20 states. Promotes a major hunger event each semester, assists students starting hunger groups and serves as a clearinghouse for new project ideas and activities of local groups.

Network, 806 Rhode Island Avenue, N.E., Washington, DC 20018, (202) 526-4070

A Catholic social justice lobby focusing particularly on the needs of the poor and the powerless. Publication lists available which include seminars and workshops.

Oxfam America, 115 Broadway, Boston, MA 02116, (617) 482-1211

Private non-profit international relief and development organization. Resources and organizing assistance for students setting up "Fast for a World Harvest" events on college campuses.

Partners in the Americas, 1424 K Street, NW #700, Washington, DC 20005, (202) 628-3300

Helps build relationships among people, organizations and communities in the Americas around shared interests in business, culture, sports, development, community health, etc.

Philanthropic Advisory Services Division, Council of Better Business Bureaus, Inc., 1515 Wilson Boulevard, Arlington, VA 22209, (703)276-0133

Provides information on organizations that solicit funds. Bimonthly lists of organizations generating largest number of inquiries. Detailed reports on large number of organizations.

Project Glean, Community Food Coalition, 5121 Port Chicago Highway, Concord, CA 94520, (415) 798-8666

See chapter 20 for a description of this organization's work.

Results, 245 Second Street, N.E., Washington, DC 20002, (202) 543-9340

National hunger lobbying organization with local chapters. Only national hunger lobby that is not religiously-based.

Returned Peace Corps Volunteers, P.O. Box 65294, Washington, DC 20035-5294

Local chapters provide speakers with direct experience in developing countries.

The Salvation Army, 799 Bloomfield Ave., Verona, NJ 07044, (201) 239-0606

Local offices in communities across the country. Provides direct assistance to poor and hungry people. Can advise groups on ways to organize effective, compassionate assistance ministries.

Second Harvest, 343 S. Dearborn St., Suite 516, Chicago, IL 60604, (312)341-1303

Non-profit tax-exempt corporation that solicits donated food and makes it available through a network of more than 75 food banks around the country. Sets standards for member food banks.

Seeds, 222 East Lake Drive, Decatur, GA 30030, (404) 378-3566

Magazine about hunger. Contains background information on domestic and international hunger and poverty and what groups are doing. Faith-based perspective.

SERVV Self-Help Handcrafts, 500 Main Street, P.O. Box 188, New Windsor, MD 21776, (301)635-6464

Program of the Brethren Church; cooperative relationship with Church World Service and denominational agencies. Purchases and markets handcrafts to assist in employment and socio-economic progress of people in developing world.

Social Investment Forum, 222 Lewis Wharf, Boston, MA 02110, (617) 423-6655
Publishes free guides to socially responsible brokers and funds. Members receive a listing in the directory and participate in SIF seminars and marketing efforts.

Sister Cities International, 120 South Payne Street, Alexandria, VA 22314-9998, (703) 836-3535
Provides support for linkages between communities in the United States and other nations. Their technical assistance program focuses on relationships with developing nations.

U.S. Conference of Mayors, 1620 Eye Street NW, Washington, DC 20006, (202)293-7330
Food Policy Project encourages mayors to develop municipal food policies. Published report *Municipal Food Policies: How Five Cities Are Improving the Availability of Quality Food for Those in Need* in October of 1985.

World Hunger Education Service, 1317 G Street, N.W., Washington, DC 20005, (202) 347-4441
Facilitates the exchange of information and insights on world food and development issues. Publishes "Hunger Notes" newsletter. Extensive collection of printed and audiovisual educational resources available.

World Hunger Year, 261 W. 35th Street, Room 1402, New York, NY 10001, (212) 629-8850
Dedicated to the reality that "every year is world hunger year until hunger is ended." Publishes "Food Monitor," a bi-monthly magazine on hunger and "Hungerline Reports."

YMCA, International Division, 101 North Wacker Dr., Chicago, IL 60606, (312) 269-0511
Promotes linkages between YWCA's in developing countries and those in Europe and North America.

Authors

Kimberly Bobo is the author of *Lives Matter: A Handbook for Christian Organizing*. Former Director of Organizing for Bread for the World, she is currently on the staff of the Midwest Academy in Chicago.

Jan Buckingham is Associate Editor of Seeds.

Mary Jo Dellinger coordinates the shelter for women and children at First Presbyterian Church in Atlanta, Georgia.

Jo-Ann Eccher is Director of Project Bread Hunger Hotline in Boston where she coordinates a statewide food stamp outreach program.

Joan Flanagan is author of *The Grass Roots Fundraising Book*. She writes and consults on fundraising for grassroots organizations.

Gary Gunderson, co-founder and former Executive Director of Seeds, helped found the sister city project between Decatur, Georgia, and Bousse and Ouahigouya in Burkino Faso, West Africa.

Callie Hutchison is Coordinator of the Tennessee Hunger Coalition, a statewide organization that does advocacy, organizing and community education.

George Johnson is Pastor of Our Savior's Lutheran Church in Circle Pines, Minnesota, and is former Director of the Hunger Program of the American Lutheran Church.

Louis Knowles is Executive Director of the Alternative Investment Project of the Council on Foundations in Washington, D.C., and a frequent contributor to *Seeds* Magazine.

Susan McCarter is Presiding Bishop's Fund Representative for the Episcopal Diocese of Atlanta and former Seeds Business Manager.

Walter L. Owensby is Associate Director of the Washington Office of the Presbyterian Church (U.S.A.).

Tom Peterson is Editor of *Seeds* Magazine.

Patricia Houck Sprinkle is author of *Hunger: Understanding the Crisis through Games, Dramas and Songs* and is Chair of the Covenant World Relief Commission of the Evangelical Covenant Church.

Leslie Withers is former Director of Education for Seeds. She serves as a consultant and workshop leader for groups dealing with hunger, justice and peace.

Subscribe to Seeds

For 10 years **Seeds** has told the moving stories of people in the front-line struggle against hunger— from women in India starting a credit co-op to church members ladling soup for the U.S. homeless.

Seeds offers analysis of domestic and world poverty issues as well as practical information—from groups that need overseas volunteers to how to start a food bank. Plus profiles, news updates, reviews, cartoons and reflections to feed the spirit.

You'll meet well-known people—Jimmy Carter, Liv Ullmann, other recognized experts and prize-winning journalists—and those whose only credentials are a warm heart and survival amidst suffering.
